# THE STRAND BOOK OF.......
# MEMORABLE MAXIMS

First published 2009 by Strand Publishing UK,
Golden Cross House, 8 Duncannon Street, Strand,
London WC2N 4JF

E-mail address: info@strandpublishing.co.uk
Internet address: www.strandpublishing.co.uk

**Paperback ISBN 978-1-907340-00-0**

# THE STRAND BOOK OF......
# MEMORABLE MAXIMS

# LIST OF AUTHORS

| | |
|---|---|
| CHARLES DARWIN | 1809-1882 |
| RENÉ DESCARTES | 1596-1650 |
| BENJAMIN DISRAELI | 1804-1881 |
| JOHN DONNE | 1572-1631 |
| JOHN DRYDEN | 1631-1700 |
| | |
| MEISTER ECKHART | c. 1260-c. 1327 |
| ALBERT EINSTEIN | 1879-1955 |
| THOMAS STEARNS ELIOT | 1888-1965 |
| RALPH WALDO EMERSON | 1803-1882 |
| FRIEDRICH ENGELS | 1820-1895 |
| EPICTETUS | c. 50-120 |
| | |
| FRANÇOIS de FÉNELON | 1651-1715 |
| EDWARD FITZGERALD | 1809-1883 |
| ANATOLE FRANCE | 1844-1924 |
| BENJAMIN FRANKLIN | 1706-1790 |
| FELIX FRANKFURTER | 1882-1965 |
| SIGMUND FREUD | 1856-1939 |
| | |
| JOSÉ ORTEGA y GASSET | 1883-1955 |
| EDWARD GIBBON | 1737-1794 |
| WILLIAM GLADSTONE | 1809-1898 |
| JOHANN von GOETHE | 1749-1832 |
| OLIVER GOLDSMITH | 1728-1774 |
| FRANCISCO JOSÉ DE GOYA | 1746-1828 |
| | |
| MARQUESS of HALIFAX | 1633-1695 |
| G W F HEGEL | 1770-1831 |
| HERACLEITUS | c.540-c.480 B.C. |
| GEORGE HERBERT | 1593-1633 |
| JOHN HEYWOOD | c. 1497-c. 1580 |
| HIPPOCRATES | c.460-c.400 B.C. |
| OLIVER WENDELL HOLMES | 1841-1935 |
| HORACE | 65-8 B.C. |
| VICTOR HUGO | 1802-1885 |

| | |
|---|---|
| THOMAS HENRY HUXLEY | 1825-1895 |
| WILLIAM JAMES | 1842-1910 |
| THOMAS JEFFERSON | 1743-1826 |
| JEROME | c. 342-420 |
| SAMUEL JOHNSON | 1709-1784 |
| CARL GUSTAV JUNG | 1875-1961 |
| | |
| THOMAS À KEMPIS | 1380-1471 |
| SÖREN KIERKEGAARD | 1813-1855 |
| KARL KRAUS | 1874-1936 |
| PETER KROPOTKIN | 1842-1921 |
| | |
| CHARLES LAMB | 1775-1834 |
| PETER M LATHAM | 1789-1875 |
| LEO XIII | 1810-1903 |
| ALAIN DE LILLE | died 1202 |
| ABRAHAM LINCOLN | 1809-1865 |
| JOHN LOCKE | 1632-1704 |
| JAMES RUSSELL LOWELL | 1819-1891 |
| LUCRETIUS | 99-55 B.C. |
| MARTIN LUTHER | 1483-1546 |
| JOHN LYLY | c. 1554-1606 |
| | |
| JOSEPH DE MAISTRE | 1753-1821 |
| THOMAS MALTHUS | 1766-1834 |
| MARCUS MANILIUS | Ist century AD |
| MAO TSE-TUNG | 1893-1976 |
| CHRISTOPHER MARLOWE | 1564-1593 |
| KARL MARX | 1818-1883 |
| ABRAHAM MASLOW | 1908-1970 |
| JULES MICHELET | 1798-1874 |
| JOHN STUART MILL | 1806-1873 |
| MOLIÈRE | 1622-1673 |
| MICHEL de MONTAIGNE | 1533-1592 |
| MONTESQUIEU | 1689-1755 |
| JOHN MORLEY | 1838-1923 |

| | |
|---|---|
| JOHN HENRY NEWMAN | 1801-1890 |
| REINHOLD NIEBUHR | 1892-1971 |
| FRIEDRICH NIETZSCHE | 1844-1900 |
| | |
| OVID | 43.B.C.-A.D.c 18 |
| | |
| BLAISE PASCAL | 1623-1662 |
| GEORGE S PATTON | 1885-1945 |
| PETRARCH | 1304-1374 |
| PHAEDRUS | fl. c. AD 8 |
| GAIUS PETRONIUS | died AD 66 |
| PLUTARCH | 46-120 |
| PLINY THE YOUNGER | c. 61-c. 112 |
| ALEXANDER POPE | 1688-1744 |
| MATTHEW PRIOR | 1664-1721 |
| PIERRE JOSEPH PROUDHON | 1809-1865 |
| | |
| FRANÇOIS RABELAIS | c. 1494-1553 |
| JOHN RAY | 1627-1705 |
| SIR JOSHUA REYNOLDS | 1723-1792 |
| LA ROCHEFOUCAULD | 1613-1680 |
| FERNANDO DE ROJAS | c. 1465-c. 1538 |
| FRANKLIN D ROOSEVELT | 1882-1945 |
| THEODORE ROOSEVELT | 1858-1918 |
| JEAN JACQUES ROUSSEAU | 1712-1778 |
| JOHN RUSKIN | 1819-1900 |
| BERTRAND RUSSELL | 1872-1970 |
| | |
| SALLUST | 86-34 B.C. |
| GUILLAUME de SALLUSTE | 1544-1590 |
| GEORGE SAND | 1804-1876 |
| GEORGE SANTAYANA | 1863-1952 |
| JEAN-PAUL SARTRE | 1905-1980 |
| SENECA | c. 4 B.C.-A.D. 65 |
| JOHANN von SCHILLER | 1759-1805 |
| ARTHUR SCHOPENHAUER | 1788-1860 |

| | |
|---|---|
| WILLIAM SHAKESPEARE | 1564-1616 |
| GEORGE BERNARD SHAW | 1856-1950 |
| SIDNEY SMITH | 1771-1845 |
| HERBERT SPENCER | 1820-1903 |
| EDMUND SPENSER | 1552-1599 |
| BARUCH SPINOZA | 1632-1677 |
| ADLAI STEVENSON | 1900-1965 |
| ROBERT LOUIS STEVENSON | 1850-1894 |
| JONATHAN SWIFT | 1667-1745 |
| PUBLILIUS SYRUS | Ist century B.C. |
| | |
| TERENCE | c. 190-159 B.C. |
| TERTULLIAN | c. 160-240 |
| HENRY DAVID THOREAU | 1817-1862 |
| LEO TOLSTOY | 1828-1910 |
| MARK TWAIN | 1835-1910 |
| JOHN TYNDALL | 1820-1893 |
| | |
| FLAVIUS VEGETIUS | $4^{th}$ century A.D. |
| VIRGIL | 70-19 B.C. |
| VOLTAIRE | 1694-1778 |
| | |
| JOHN WEBSTER | c. 1580-c. 1625 |
| DUKE OF WELLINGTON | 1769-1852 |
| ALFRED N WHITEHEAD | 1861-1947 |
| OSCAR WILDE | 1854-1900 |
| WILLIAM WORDSWORTH | 1770-1850 |
| WILLIAM OF WYKEHAM | 1324-1404 |
| | |
| WILLIAM BUTLER YEATS | 1865-1939 |

# INTRODUCTION

We have been warned that nobody reads a Preface, Introduction, Prologue, or whatever name you choose for the editors' or authors' introductory words. That's as may be; yet such an introduction is necessary, if only for the discerning. It is not enough, surely, to throw together the maxims of all the ages, or a selection of them, and not explain the guiding principles behind the selection. . The reader has the right to know what those principles are.

This is a book that presents quotations, but it is not a dictionary of quotations. This is a book of maxims. And there we encounter the first difficulty: what, exactly, is a maxim? It is one of the glories of the English language, its richness, and its variety, that no two words are ever exact synonyms. English is derived from many languages. Words have derived from the directness of Anglo-Saxon, Danish and German; from Greek and Latin, whence have come the words we need for learning generally, and for the sciences, medicine, law and ecclesiastical business specifically. This process continues daily, as words are added from Hindi and Urdu, from Bengali and Swahili, from Afrikaans and Arabic, and the newer languages of computer-speak and E mail communications.

Languages cannot remain static. All, as Heracleitus stated two and a half thousand years ago, is flux, nothing stands still. Thus, over the centuries, there have been many words that indicate or are related to the wisdom that humankind accumulates and wishes to pass on to younger generations. This wisdom has often been preserved in brief and pithy forms. Because there are no exact synonyms, it is difficult to differentiate between a proverb, an aphorism, an epigram and a maxim. Certain statements may, of course, be all four.

This is a book of maxims. The following have been our guiding principles.

- Each maxim must exemplify a general truth.

- Each one must be brief, pithy, to the point.

- The statement must have enduring insight into the human condition.

- Only writers who are safely dead and out of copyright have been chosen.

Unless the maxim contains a general truth, it cannot safely be considered a maxim. What passes for interest in one generation may fail totally to pass muster in another. It is not claimed that truth is absolute, but there must, for the maxim to be admitted, be an element of abiding truth.

The nature of a maxim is in its brevity, that it may be remembered easily and passed on orally as well as in written form. Some of the best maxims are not only brief, but also well balanced. The writers of the eighteenth century knew all about balance, as did the best of the

Romans, on whom the Augustans modelled themselves. Some writers, not least politicians and philosophers, are very long-winded. An example is Nietzsche. Where he is pithy, he has been included; otherwise, he has been rigorously excluded, no matter what the value of his writing.

Brevity is essential, or the quotation becomes something other than a maxim. Several writers fall down badly in this regard. Many politicians and philosophers have had to be excluded for their verbosity.

Insight into the human condition does not come easily. It is, all too often, the product of age and experience. Thus, many of the maxims contained in this book are the products of writers in retirement, looking back, reflecting, perhaps even warning. We have been rigorous in our exclusion of the merely hortatory; and this explains why so few politicians appear. Gladstone, like Nietzsche, had many interesting comments to make, but, like the philosopher, he too was a Victorian windbag.

Age and experience may lead a person to be rather cynical. We have not excluded on the grounds of cynicism alone – had we done so, the estimable Sir Francis Bacon would not be here, nor Lord Chesterfield. The predominant mood is not cynicism, however, but, rather, pessimism and lack of hope for human beings as a species. This, perhaps, is the result of growing older and reflecting on life, manners and man's injustice and inhumanity to man.

Writers may be considered important, and prominent in the canon, but unless they have maxims to offer they have been excluded. Such an example is Charles Dickens. No teller of tales in English has afforded greater pleasure than Dickens, yet he cannot be found in this collection, because he rarely, if ever, dealt in maxims. The same is true of Henry James, who has also afforded great pleasure to readers, though not, we venture to think, in the same volume or amount as Charles Dickens.

The first maxims were probably written by Hippocrates, and were medical precepts. "For extreme illnesses, extreme treatments are most fitting," is one of his. This has come down to us today in various forms, of which perhaps the best known is the maxim that extreme diseases require desperate measures, or as Shakespeare memorably says in Hamlet: "Diseases desperate grown / By desperate appliances are relieved / Or not at all."

The reader may know a maxim in a different form from the one we have given in these pages. As Ben Jonson said of Shakespeare, we have small Latin and less Greek. In addition, maxims change by being given oral currency. If you believe strongly that what we have given is incorrect, contact us by letter or E-mail. We state the latter because it is fast and informal. This book may deal in the eternal verities, but that does not mean we are ignorant of modern technology and means of communication. Where we become convinced of error, be sure a correction will be made in subsequent printings of this book, and due acknowledgement graciously made.

How does this collection differ from other collections of epigrams, aphorisms and proverbs? First, in that we have excluded proverbs wherever possible. Very few rolling stones gather moss in this collection, though the original of that maxim, by Publilius Syrus, is included. Others who have collected proverbs need not feel threatened.

You will find few maxims from the Bible, none from the Qu'ran or other works of religion. There are good reasons for these deliberate omissions. Those books of scripture are packed with maxims and they would engulf our short collection, sink the ship before it could get out to sea. Such an anthology would be valid, but we shall not prepare it. This must not be taken as antipathy toward religion but, rather, a concern to exclude exhortation. The second consideration refers to copyright, or to which version of the scriptures to quote. Let those who glory in the beautiful language of the Authorised Version go to the Bible itself.

We have included more science than is perhaps usual in these collections. While the literary may still predominate, we feel we have achieved a proper balance. Human life deals with more than poetry, though poetry is essential to human life. Thus, John Tyndall rubs shoulders with John Ruskin, and Herbert Spencer with George S Patton. The law and politics are admitted: some of the finest maxims have been written by eminent jurists, while even politicians - rightly despised today – were not always uniformly venal in the past. You will find Thomas Jefferson and Franklin Roosevelt within these pages, as well as Felix Frankfurter and Oliver Wendell Holmes.

Those four men are all Americans. This collection is not of English maxims, but of maxims in English, even if many, especially the Greeks and Romans, are necessarily in translation. And most of those included are male, because, alas, that was the way of things in the past. Because we have chosen only authors who are dead, the feminist renaissance of the past three decades cannot be represented. That may be something to address in a companion volume.

The language of the past was predominantly male and avowedly sexist. This we deprecate, because we are the children of our own times. Nevertheless, we have not foolishly attempted to update dead writers. In most cases the results would be ludicrous. John Donne did not state that *No person is an island unto theirselves*; nor did Alexander Pope declare that *the Proper study of Humankind is persons.*

Use this collection in any way you like. Perhaps you would like to take Lavater's advice, written about 1788, as number 643 in his collection of *Aphorisms on Man.*

*"If you mean to know yourself, interline such of these aphorisms as affect you agreeably in reading, and set a mark to such as left a sense of uneasiness with you; and then show your copy to whom you please."*

By all means underline your copy; set a mark against any that cause you unease. Then drop us an E-mail. We promise to respond to every comment or suggestion, save those that are extremely vulgar or unnecessarily abusive. In particular, we shall consider carefully, for inclusion later, suggestions for maxims we do not know

Be interactive, by all means, but don't follow Lavater's advice and show your copy to whom you please. Let them go out and purchase their own copy.

The Editors

Hold faithfulness and sincerity as first principles.

Fine words and an insinuating appearance are seldom associated with true virtue.

Learning without thought is labour lost; thought without learning is dangerous.

The cautious seldom err.


## CONFUCIUS
## 551-479 B.C.

Confucius was Chinese. The name by which he is commonly known in the West is a Latinised form of Kung Fu-tse, the master or philosopher.

Though principally a philosopher, Confucius wanted to see a practical application of his principles. He understood that in order to relieve the sufferings of very poor people, some form of governmental action is required.Confucius spent many years seeking a post that would

We cannot step into the same river twice.

All is flux; nothing stays still.

Nothing endures except change.

Much learning does not teach understanding.

## HERACLEITUS
## c.540-c.480 B.C.

Heracleitus or Heraclitus was a Greek philosopher and cosmologist. He believed that the universe, the whole of Creation, was in a constant state of change and movement. Fire was the fundamental material of the universe and this accounted for the constant movement and change.

Nothing is known of his life; even the dates of birth and death are disputed. What we know of his work has been filtered through other writers. What is not in dispute is the wisdom contained in his maxims. Nobody sensible now disputes that everything is in motion, even the seemingly solid chair on which we sit.

The life so short, the craft so long to learn.

Healing is a matter of time but it is sometimes a matter of opportunity.

For extreme illnesses, extreme treatments are most fitting.

Many admire, few know.

Prayer is indeed good, but while calling on the gods a man should himself lend a hand.

## HIPPOCRATES
## c.460-c400 B.C.

A Greek, Hippocrates was born on the island of Kos, where he practised as a physician. He stressed the importance of cleanliness for patient and doctor alike. He advocated the virtue of moderation in diet and in life generally. Lack of balance in the body leads to disease. Fresh clean air was considered by him to be necessary for good health.

He has been called "The Father of Medicine."

Charity begins at home.

While there is life, there's hope.

He is wise who tries everything before resorting to arms.


## TERENCE
## c. 190-159 B.C.

Publius Terentius Afer was born in Carthage, in modern Tunisia, North Africa. He was taken to Rome as a slave by a senator. The master was impressed by his slave's intelligence and had him educated. Later, the lad was freed and he adopted the name of the senator, Terentius.

Terence became a dramatist and specialised in comic plays written in verse. His work has been influential because he wedded together Greek and Roman models for play construction. Those who know Latin well praise the purity of his verse.

Let the punishment match the offence.

The mind of each man is the man himself.

Laws are inoperative in war.

The good of the people is the chief law.

## CICERO
## 106-43 B.C.

As orator and politician, Marcus Tullius Cicero was deeply involved in some of the most tumultuous times of Roman history. When his party was not in the ascendant, Cicero was exiled from Rome, and in those periods he devoted himself to writing, especially speeches. His orations were often powerful and influenced the actions of his fellow citizens.

He took the side of Pompey against Julius Caesar, but was pardoned after Pompey's defeat. After the murder of Julius Caesar, in which he was not implicated, Cicero supported Octavian against Antony. Cicero was murdered, probably by agents of Antony.

Men willingly believe what they wish.

## JULIUS CAESAR
## 100-44 B.C.

Julius Caesar is one of the best-known of Romans, because of the play written by Shakespeare, and because for hundreds of years schoolboys were forced to read and translate his account of his several conquests, not least the conquest of Gaul, or modern France.

Of patrician birth, Julius held many positions, including being governor in various parts of the Roman Empire. Always ambitious, he was eventually one third of a powerful triumvirate along with Crassus and Pompey. When Crassus died, Julius and Pompey struggled for power and Julius emerged victorious. He was made dictator for a ten year period. (He was opposed by Cicero, as always a staunch republican.) After less than two years in power, Julius Caesar was murdered by Brutus and his fellow conspirators in March 44 B.C.

Nothing can be created from nothing.

Nature works by means of bodies unseen.

## LUCRETIUS
## 99-55 B.C.

Titus Lucretius Carus was a Roman poet and philosopher. Little is known of him or his life apart from the poem *De rerum natura* (*On the Nature of Things*.). He espoused the theory of the Greek Epicurus that matter is made of atoms. He argued that there is a human soul but that it perishes with the body. There are gods but they are powerless to intervene in human events.

The atomic theory that he propounds is very modern. No single thing is created from nothing; and no single thing can be reduced to nothing. Atoms vary in shape, size and weight. Ultimately, all things are moving atoms. Change can be explained by the addition or reduction of atoms in a group.

To like and dislike the same things; that is indeed true friendship.

The splendid achievements of the intellect are everlasting.

Every man is the architect of his own fortune.

## SALLUST
## 86-34 B.C.

Gaius Sallustius Crispus was a Roman senator. He is remembered as the political historian who recorded the events at the end of the Republic and the transition to an Empire. As well as being an historian of events, he was deeply involved in politics as governor, senator and commander of Julius Caesar's legions. When Caesar was assassinated, Sallust retired to compose his history of the tumultuous events in which he had participated and to which he had often been witness.

Your descendants shall gather your fruits.

Time flies, never to return.

## VIRGIL
## 70-19 B.C.

When Virgil was twenty years old, Julius Caesar seized power in the Roman republic. The next decade was a period of civil wars. The eventual victor of these wars was Augustus Caesar. Augustus brought in a period of peace.

Virgil, like his friend Horace, steered clear of direct political involvement, but he received encouragement and support from Maecenas, a minister in Augustus' government who was a patron of the arts. Poor health saved him from a military life. Thus, he was able to spend his adult life on his farm, writing poetry.

*The Aeneid* took eleven years to write. It tells the story of Aeneas, who escaped from Troy at the end of the Trojan Wars, and became the legendary founder of Rome

Those who aim at great deeds must also suffer greatly.

## MARCUS CRASSUS
## c. 108 -53 B.C.

Crassus was a Roman army officer who was deeply involved in politics in the final years of the Roman republic. The pinnacle of his power was as one part of the triumvirate with Pompey and Julius Caesar.

He is remembered as the general who crushed the revolt of slaves led by Spartacus. Later, in his attempt to gain military glory, and enhance his political fortunes, Crassus invaded Parthia, to the east of Syria. At the time he was governor of Syria. Crassus was defeated, captured and put to death.

He aimed at great deeds, and suffered accordingly.

Whoever cultivates the golden mean avoids both poverty and envy.

It is the mountain top that the lightning strikes.

Force without wisdom falls of its own weight.

## HORACE
## 65-8 B.C.

Horace was the son of a freed slave. He received a good education, both in Italy and in Greece. Later he became a tribune in the army, which was rare for the son of a freed slave. He was a supporter of Augustus in the civil wars that affected Rome both before and after the assassination of Julius Caesar.

Horace was rewarded with the gift from Maecenas of a farm in the Sabine hills close to Rome. Working from his farm, Horace wrote a great deal of poetry. The best-known collections are the *Odes*. In these he writes of, and sings the praises of, nature, friendship, love and wine. Always he praises moderation. Like Virgil, he valued the peaceful Augustan years that followed a long period of civil strife. Horace was humane, tolerant and kind.

We can learn even from our enemies.

Time devours all things.

If you wish to be loved, be loveable.

## OVID
## 43 B.C.-A.D. c. 18

Poets may separate themselves from politics, but they cannot keep away from love. Poetry speaks of the eternal truths, of which love is one. Publius Ovidius Naso is the arch-apostle of love.

Being born into an upper-class family, Ovid received a good education, although he rebelled against what he considered sterile rhetorical exercises. He travelled, especially to Athens, where he learned a great deal about Greek landscape and Greek mythology.

His best-known work is *The Metamorphoses*, a long poem recounting myths and legends. With this work he achieved fame and honour. Then, with a swiftness that echoes Greek tragedy, Ovid fell. He was banished for life for having an affair with the Emperor's daughter.

Things are not always what they seem.

Once it is lost, not even Jupiter can bring back an opportunity.

## PHAEDRUS
## fl. c. AD 8

Very little is known of Phaedrus, except that he was born a slave in Macedonia, went to Rome, was employed as a servant in the household of Augustus, and was made a free man. He wrote fables in the manner of Aesop.

Man is a reasoning animal.

It is a rough road that leads to the heights of greatness.

Fire is the test of gold; and adversity of strong men.

There is no great genius without a touch of madness.

## SENECA
## c. 4 B.C.-A.D. 65

Seneca the Younger entered politics and was almost killed by the emperor Caligula (the one who made his horse a Consul).

In A.D. 41 Seneca was banished to the island of Corsica. His crime was an affair with the emperor's niece. After eight years he was recalled to Rome. He married a wealthy woman and developed political friendships. He became tutor to Nero, the future emperor. In A.D. 65 Seneca was accused of being implicated in a rebellion. He was ordered to commit suicide. He obeyed.

A good reputation is more valuable than money.

You should hammer your iron when it is glowing hot.

There are some remedies worse than the disease.

The fear of death is more to be dreaded than death itself.

A rolling stone gathers no moss.

We desire nothing so much as what we ought not to have.

Not every question deserves an answer.

Never thrust your own sickle into someone else's corn.

Every day should be spent as if it were our last.

**PUBLILIUS SYRUS**
**Ist century B.C.**

Little is known of Syrus, apart from his many maxims.

At birth, our death is sealed; and our end is consequent upon our beginning.


## MARCUS MANILIUS
## Ist century AD

Manilius is a minor figure. Lucretius, Ovid and Virgil influenced him.

He wrote *Astronomica*, a poem concerned with astronomy and astrology. It was never completed. It appears that the best parts of the poem are when Manilius allows himself to digress from the topic. The maxim presented here is typical. It clearly influenced T S Eliot when he was writing *The Four Quartets*. For proof see the beginning of *East Coker* and Section V of *Little Gidding*.

One good turn deserves another.

A man must have his faults.

Beauty and wisdom are rarely found together.

## GAIUS PETRONIUS
### died AD 66

During the reign of Augustus, in the first century, Gaius was prefect of Egypt. He tightened Rome's grip on the province and extended it to the Nile's first cataract. He was probably not the first man to notice that beauty and wisdom are rarely found together, nor the last. When beauty and wisdom are found together, however, that is something to behold.

A liar needs to have a good memory.


## QUINTILIAN
## 35-95

Marcus Fabius Quintilianus was born in Spain but spent his adult life in Rome, teaching the art of rhetoric. He advocated that rhetoric should be plain and sincere. Few politicians have followed this advice.

Bad news travels fast and far.

When the lights are out, all women are fair.

## PLUTARCH
## 46-120

A Greek by birth, Plutarch studied mathematics and philosophy. Later he travelled to Rome to work. It is possible that he enjoyed the company of Trajan and Hadrian, both to serve as emperors. Tradition has it that Hadrian made Plutarch the procurator of Greece, but there is no evidence for this.

What is certain is that Plutarch wrote the lives of Greek and Roman statesmen, orators and other public figures. His descriptions of their deeds and characters were later to be adopted as models of behaviour. Sir Thomas North translated Plutarch's Lives into English in 1579. Shakespeare used the *Lives* for material when writing his Roman plays.

Plutarch remained popular until the nineteenth century. The evening before Charlotte Corday stabbed Marat in his bath, she spent the time reading Plutarch.

Only the educated are free.


## EPICTETUS
## c. 50-120

Little is known of this man. Even his name is the Greek word for *acquired*. He was possibly born a slave. His life appears to have been spent fighting ill-health and lameness.

He left no books behind. A pupil wrote down his philosophy. In his teaching, Epictetus followed Socrates and the Stoics. God has given us a will. We receive ideas from God. What matters is how we deal with those ideas. He encouraged people to refrain from self-interest and thus promote the common good.

Honesty is praised, and starves.

It is not easy for men to rise whose qualities are thwarted by poverty.

You should pray for a sound mind in a sound body.

## JUVENAL
## c. 50-c. 130

Little is known of Juvenal, but much is known of his sixteen *Satires*. They hit many targets. Juvenal is bitter and bitchy. He attacks folly, arrogance and cruelty. Vain women are not spared, and their sexual depravity in contemporary Rome is laid bare. Male homosexuals are also the recipients of his lash.

Many of his sayings are still quoted, often by politicians who have never heard the name of Juvenal. "Bread and circuses" is one example. So too is: "Who will guard the guards themselves?"

Juvenal was made bitter by exile and by the depravity and corruption of the times in which he lived.

An object in one's possession seldom retains the charm it had in pursuit.

## PLINY THE YOUNGER
## c. 61-c. 112

Pliny was a successful legal advocate and public administrator. He achieved many high posts in imperial Rome. Now he is chiefly remembered for his letters.

He was a careful man, and never strayed too far from the official line. However, he did suggest that while Christians may be a sect, they were not advocates of vicious practices.

Like many successful men, Pliny comes across as complacent.

The universe is change; our life is what our thoughts make it.

Death, like birth, is a secret of Nature.

Very little is needed to make a happy life.

## MARCUS AURELIUS
## 121-180

Marcus came from a successful Roman family. At the age of seventeen, Marcus was chosen as a likely successor to the throne. He did not take the position until he was forty, but he played the political game correctly for twenty-three years.

Marcus Aurelius is not in the front rank of Roman emperors. As a thinker, he is in no rank at all. Renewed interest in the *Meditations* in recent years tells us a great deal about the shallowness of our own age.

Truth does not blush.

It is certainly no part of religion to compel religion.

## TERTULLIAN
## c. 160-240

Until the time of Tertullian, Greek was the language of Christianity. He changed it to Latin.

Born in Carthage, in modern Tunisia, Tertullian was a probably a lawyer in Rome. Later he was converted to the new religion. Little else is known of him personally.

He soon became dissatisfied with what he saw as the laxity of Roman Christians, and joined a North African sect. He eventually broke with them too and formed his own group. Because of his apostasy he has largely been written out of the Christian record, as Plekhanov and then Trotsky were airbrushed from the Communist history falsified by Lenin and Stalin. Tertullian remains, however, an influential and important founding father.

Love is not to be purchased, and affection has no price.

The friendship that can cease has never been real.

It is easier to mend neglect than to quicken love.

Love knows nothing of order.

No athlete is crowned save in the sweat of his brow.

## ST JEROME
## c. 342-420

Jerome was born somewhere in the Balkans but educated in Rome. He travelled a great deal. He lived in the Syrian desert for two years as a hermit.

His greatest claim to be remembered is in his translation of the Bible into Latin, the *Vulgate*. This work had a profound influence on Christian thought and opinion until the end of the Middle Ages in the West.

Necessity has no law.

Anger is a weed; hate is the tree.

## ST AUGUSTINE
**354-430**

St Augustine of Hippo – not to be confused with Augustine, first archbishop of Canterbury – was born in North Africa, in modern Algeria. While he was studying philosophy, he favoured the pre-Christian Greeks, but was converted to the new religion at the age of twenty-eight. He was baptised by Jerome.

He is remembered as an influential Christian philosopher who rooted out various heresies. He wrote his *Confessions* and later the very influential *The City of God*.

Let him who desires peace, prepare for war.


**FLAVIUS VEGETIUS**
**4<sup>th</sup> century A.D.**

Vegetetius had little influence in his own time, when the Roman Empire was crumbling.

His writing on siegecraft was studied in the Middle Ages, and put to practical use. He advocated the use of armed infantry, constant drill, severe discipline to keep order, and a study of landforms to choose the best sites for a battle.

It can be said that he turned medieval warfare from a pastime for aristocrats into a powerful engine for nations to assert their will.

In every adversity of fortune, to have been happy is the worst kind of misfortune.

## BOETHIUS
## 480-424

Most students come across Boethius, if at all, as a footnote in their imperfect reading of Chaucer's *Canterbury Tales*. He was, however, rather more than a footnote in his time and deserves to be rescued from the mists of antiquity.

He was active in Roman politics, having been born into a powerful Christian family. He translated Greek texts into Latin, and attempted to reconcile ancient Greek philosophies with Christianity. In this way he was very influential on the formation of the Middle Ages.

He rose to be consul but then fell from favour and was imprisoned. While in prison he wrote *The Consolations of Philosophy*, which was a well-known text in medieval times. Boethius was executed, accused of practising magic.

Hell is full of good intentions or desires.

## ST BERNARD
## 1091-1153

Bernard of Clairvaux, a saint of the Christian church, was born in Dijon, where the mustard comes from, and died in Clairvaux, where champagne comes from.

Bernard was a monk and mystic, the confidant of five popes, important in civil and ecclesiastical councils, and promoter of the Second Crusade. The crusade was a failure but Bernard had done enough to be canonised as a saint of the church.

Do not think gold all that shines like gold.


## ALAIN DE LILLE
## died 1202

The editors would welcome facts about Alain's life. It appears that he was also known as Alanus de Insulis, if that is any help.

He is included in these pages because his maxim echoes those written by other, better-known people.

All that glitters, or all that is yellow, is not gold was a common proverb in the Middle Ages, and may originally have been a translation from Aristotle. It is found in Chaucer's *Canterbury Tales*

It is probably best known from Shakespeare's *The Merchant of Venice* (Act 2 sc. vii*): All that glisters in not gold.* Glisters is commonly misquoted as glitters, even by those who should know better.

In silence man can most readily preserve his integrity.

Our works do not ennoble us, but we must ennoble our works.

## MEISTER ECKHART
### c. 1260-c. 1327

Eckhart von Hochheim was a medieval monk of the Dominican order. He spent much of his life opposing the Franciscan order.

At the age of sixty he was appointed as professor in Cologne. The archbishop of Cologne, who was a Franciscan, accused Eckhart of heresy. Eckhart was condemned by the pope, but died before further action could be taken He is considered to be a precursor of Protestantism, and also of Existentialism.

Rarely do great beauty and great virtue dwell together.

## PETRARCH
## 1304-1374

Francesco Petrarch's parents were from Florence in Italy but he himself was born in Arezzo. Later the family moved to Avignon, in southern France.

Although he was a scholar with great knowledge of classical texts, Petrarch is mainly remembered as a lyric poet and for his chaste love of *Laura*. He first saw her in church in 1327, and loved her until his death in 1374. No one has been able to say who *Laura* was. Petrarch may have asked her to be is mistress but, if he did, she refused.

Petrarch believed that the present must be informed by the past. His study of classical texts paved the way for the Renaissance.

He died in his study, at night, while working. When he was found, he had his head on an open copy of Virgil.

Manners maketh man.

## WILLIAM OF WYKEHAM
## 1324-1404

William of Wykeham was chancellor to two kings, Edward III and Richard II. He was also bishop of Winchester.

In 1380 he founded New College, Oxford, and two years later he founded Winchester College as a feeder institution for New College.

Among Goethe's Proverbs in Prose is: *A man's manners are a mirror in which he shows his portrait,* which is perhaps a more felicitous way of making the point. It is in William's form that the maxim is most often quoted.

Love is blind.

## GEOFFREY CHAUCER
## 1343-1400

Chaucer is best remembered for *The Canterbury Tales*, his collection of tales ostensibly told by pilgrims on their way from Southwark in London to the shrine of Thomas à Becket in Canterbury. In the tales Chaucer presents a cross-section of medieval society, and presents most people in a satirical fashion. His work was influential to such an extent that his form of southern English became the basis for Standard English.

As well as The *Canterbury Tales,* Chaucer wrote *Romance of the Rose*, an allegorical poem that presents a depiction of courtly love.

Man proposes but God disposes.

First keep the peace within yourself and then you can also bring peace to others.

## THOMAS À KEMPIS
## 1380-1471

Thomas was a German monk of the Augustinian order. He was probably the author of *The Imitation of Christ*, though this book may have been the work of several monks within the religious group known as Brethren of the Common Life. The brethren were devoted to education and to care of the poor.

The *Imitation* is written in a simple, accessible style. Thomas stresses austerity but not extreme asceticism, spirituality in life rather than materialism, and he avoids an excess of mysticism. Thomas spent seventy years in a single monastery at Zwolle in the Netherlands.

The first step toward madness is to think oneself wise.

Riches do not make one rich, but busy.

When one door closes, fortune will usually open another.

## FERNANDO DE ROJAS
## 1465-c. 1538

Rojas was a Spanish writer, probably a Jew who converted to Christianity. In 1499 he published a tale in the form of a dialogue. under the title *Comedia de Calixto y Melibea*. It tells of a procuress, Celestina, and the tale became commonly known as *La Celestina*.

This is the first example in Spanish, and indeed in Europe, of a novel that combines romance and realism. There is in the tale a successful combination of psychological analysis and dramatic conflict, and in this way de Rojas had a great influence on the development of the novel in Europe.

There is no more lovely, friendly and charming relationship, communion or company than a good marriage.

## MARTIN LUTHER
## 1483-1546

There is no doubt that Luther is among the most influential people of the last two thousand years. He challenged the power of the Roman Catholic Church and became the founder of Protestantism. He defied the Pope in Rome and the Holy Roman Emperor too.

Luther was a difficult person and often a violent controversialist, but there is no denying his influence on the Christian world.

By reducing the power of the papacy, and changing the emphasis in Christianity from papal authority to scriptural authority, Luther opened the doors to a wider range of free thinking, and thus heralded the demise of the medieval world order. With Protestantism there came also new ways of conducting political affairs and economic business. Because of this, the northern states of Europe – the Netherlands, England, Germany – became powerful.

To laugh is proper to man.

## FRANÇOIS RABELAIS
## c. 1494-1553

A monk and a physician, Rabelais is chiefly remembered today as a powerful satirist. He is also a bawdy writer, and many cannot see beyond the bawdiness to the biting satire beneath.

Rabelais writes of two giants, father and son, Gargantua and Pantagruel. In these two books, Rabelais combines deep psychological insight, powers of observation and description, and a fluent and allusive prose style. Thus, even today the works read well, and the satire is, of course, timeless, for human nature in essence hardly changes from age to age.

Make hay when the sun shines.

The tide tarrieth no man.

A hard beginning makes a good ending.

Two heads are better than one.

One good turn asketh another.

There is no fool to the old fool.

Many hands make light work.

There is no fire without some smoke.

Enough is as good as a feast.

## JOHN HEYWOOD
### c.1497-c. 1580

Heywood was a courtier at the court of Henry V111, and was a singer and musician there.

Heywood was also a dramatist. He was among the first to move away from allegorical Biblical plays of the "Mystery" form to realistic depictions of everyday life and character.

The thing I fear most is fear.

Nothing is so firmly believed as what is least known.

The greatest thing in the world is to know how to belong to oneself.

Saying is one thing and doing is another.

## MICHEL de MONTAIGNE
## 1533-1592

In his *Essays* Montaigne developed a new, and eventually most influential, literary form. He was opposed to the religious intolerance of his day, and advocated a new humanism.

He followed the Socratic precept of "Know thyself", but found this difficult. He wrote: "If my mind could gain a foothold, I would not write essays. I would make decisions." Montaigne yearned for certainty, and failed to find it. In his musings on Being and on Nothingness, he has been seen, rightly, as a precursor of Existentialism.

Who breaks his faith, no faith is held with him.

## GUILLAUME de SALLUSTE
## 1544-1590

Author of an influential poem, *La Semaine*, about the creation of the world.

Salluste is sometimes known as Bartas, because he was Guillaume de Salluste, seigneur du Barsat. Apart from this single maxim, he is little remembered, and was not even much applauded in his own lifetime.

Absence, that common cure for love.

The proof of the pudding is in the eating.

There's no striving against the stream, and the weakest still go to the wall.

Diligence is the mother of good fortune.

## MIGUEL de CERVANTES
## 1547-1616

A soldier, Cervantes was wounded at the important and decisive battle of Lepanto, in 1571. Returning to Spain, he was captured by Barbary pirates and had to endure slavery for five years, until ransomed.

At first he tried to live as a playwright, but lacked success, and was compelled to become an inspector of taxes. He was several times thrown into prison because he cooked the books. He sank lower in society and was degraded by poverty. Then, in 1605, he achieved fame and wealth with *Don Quixote*.

Cervantes died on the same day as William Shakespeare.

Sleep after toil, port after stormy seas.
Here on earth is no sure happiness.

## EDMUND SPENSER
## 1552-1599

Spenser was in his own time honoured as a fine poet and as a master of metrical patterns.

He is now remembered chiefly for *The Faerie Queene,* a moral allegory dedicated to Elizabeth 1st.

Although Spenser was an important influence on the Romantic poets, who learned from his rich imagery and his verse craft, he is probably little read today. He is buried in Westminster Abbey.

The finest edge is made with the blunt whetstone.

A rose is sweeter in the bud than full blown.

Marriages are made in heaven and consummated on earth.

## JOHN LYLY
## c. 1554-1606

English playwright and author.

Among his work was Euphues, or the Anatomy of Wit. Because of the elaborate stylistic devices in this work, such a style became known as *euphuism*, and the term has passed into the language.

Students should be careful not to confuse euphuism with euphemism. The only thing they have in common is their derivation from Greek.

Knowledge is power.

Nothing is terrible except fear itself.

Hope is a good breakfast but it is a bad supper.

Wives are young men's mistresses, companions for middle age, and old men's nurses

A good name is like a precious ointment.

Reading maketh a full man, conference a ready man, and writing an exact man.

## FRANCIS BACON
## 1561-1626

Bacon was a man of many parts and many arts. He was a politician, civil servant, courtier, ambassador, essayist and philosopher. His influence has lasted down five centuries.

The theory, first advanced in 1785, that Bacon is the author of the plays attributed to Shakespeare, is nonsense

Hell hath no limits, nor is circumscribed
In one self place.

## CHRISTOPHER MARLOWE
## 1564-1593

Kit Marlowe remains a man of mystery.

It is known that he was born in Canterbury and was educated at Cambridge university. His relatively short life was a turbulent one. He was imprisoned for killing a man in a tavern brawl, but was cleared. He was later killed in a tavern himself, in Deptford, London. He was stabbed to death.

Marlowe was accused of atheism in a time of religious intolerance. He was certainly a government agent, and may have been an aggressive homosexual. Which of these led to his murder in Deptford is a mystery that will never be solved.

His nduring plays include: *Tamburlaine the Great, The Jew of Malta, Edward 11,* and *Dr. Faustus.*

True nobility is exempt from fear.

Delays have dangerous ends.

Hasty marriage seldom proveth well.

Talkers are no good doers.

'Tis an ill cook that cannot lick his own fingers.

The better part of valour is discretion.

Everyone can master a grief but he that has it.

Patch griefs with proverbs.

## WILLIAM SHAKESPEARE
## 1564-1616

A whole volume could be devoted to the maxims of Shakespeare. The ones above are a mere selection from many thousands.

There is nothing important to say about Shakespeare, except that he is without peer as a poet and dramatist. He belongs to the whole world.

Who are a little wise, the best fools be.

Love built on beauty, soon as beauty, dies.

No man is an island, entire of itself; every man is a piece of the continent, a part of the main.

**JOHN DONNE**
**1572-1631**

Donne is noted for both his prose writings and his verse.

He was an Anglican clergyman who became Dean of St.Paul's church in London.

After his death, Donne's work fell from favour. In the case of his poetry, we can surmise that difficulties in understanding were part of the reason for neglect.

Donne returned to critical and popular favour in the C20, when he and his group were placed together under the heading of Metaphysical poets.

Birds of a feather will gather together.

England is a paradise for women and hell for horses; Italy a paradise for horses, a hell for women.

## ROBERT BURTON
## 1577-1640

Like John Donne, an Anglican clergyman, who lived in Oxford university most of his life.

Burton devoted much time to compiling his *Anatomy of Melancholy*, which discusses the philosophical and psychological ideas of his time, especially as they relate to health and to mental illness. He seeks to define melancholy or depression and to discuss the possible causes. His work is important for its style and also for the way in which Burton condenses the knowledge of his times and former times, and is thus a useful guide for readers and scholars alike.

Dr Samuel Johnson, who often suffered from bouts of melancholy, praises Burton's work highly. It was, Johnson told Boswell, the only book that took him out of bed two hours sooner than he wished to rise.

I know death has ten thousand several doors for men to take their exits.

Vain the ambition of kings
Who seek by trophies and dead things
To leave a living name behind,
And weave but nets to catch the wind.

## JOHN WEBSTER
## c. 1580-c. 1625

John Webster is an important English tragedian, second only to William Shakespeare.

Webster's two great plays are *The Duchess of Malfi* and *The White Devil.* Both deal with the theme of revenge. They are violent, bloody and dark. The power of poetry raises them above the level of the ordinary revenge plays of the period.

In a famous poem T. S. Eliot writes: "Webster was much possessed by death/And saw the skull beneath the skin."

Hell is full of good meanings and wishings.

Where the drink goes in, there the wit goes out.

God's mill grinds slow, but sure.

Words are women, deeds are men.

Poverty is no sin.

None knows the weight of another's burden.

One hour's sleep before midnight is worth three after.

He hath no pleasure who uses it not.

Half the world knows not how the other half lives.

Life is half spent before we know what it is.

## GEORGE HERBERT
## 1593-1633

Herbert was a devotional poet and many of his poems are sung as hymns, even today.

It is not enough to have a good mind. The main thing is to use it well.

He first precept was never to accept a thing as true until I knew it as such without a single doubt.

## RENÉ DESCARTES
## 1596-1650

Descartes is among the foremost of Western philosophers. It is almost impossible to over-estimate his importance to both philosophy and science.

He was educated by Jesuits and this had the result of making him question many things, not least the nature of religious thought. In particular, he distinguished between the Mind and the Body. This duality dominated philosophy right up to the middle of the C20.

His most lasting work has proved to be *The Discourse of Method*. His influence on science and philosophy stems from his insistence on mechanistic principles.

A few honest men are better than numbers.

## OLIVER CROMWELL
## 1599-1658

Those who like Cromwell, love him with a power little short of idolatry, while those who hate him, do so with a magnificent passion. He was a farmer who by circumstances had to become a soldier. He led the parliamentary army to many successes during the great English Civil War of the C17.

He was elected to parliament at the age of twenty-nine years, and made little mark. On the outbreak of the war, Cromwell was a captain in the Parliamentary forces. He fought well at the battle of Edgehill, and within one year was second-in-command of the army.

By 1653, Cromwell was appointed Lord Protector, king in all but name. Although his years of military and political office were few, Cromwell achieved a great deal.

After his death, the Royalists hanged his remains, and for many years exhibited his head on a pole in Westminster.

A man may be in as just possession of truth as of a city, and yet be forced to surrender.

The heart of man is the place the devils dwell in: I feel sometimes a hell within myself.

There is no road or ready way to virtue.

The created world is but a small parenthesis in eternity.

## THOMAS BROWNE
## 1605-1682

Browne was a doctor. As a physician he attained no great position, preferring to practice quietly, first in Halifax, in Yorkshire, and then in Norwich, Norfolk.

As a young doctor he began to compile notebooks, a journal in which he mediated on the nature of God, nature and the position of human beings within this scheme. These notebooks formed the basis of his book *Religio Medici.*

Although Browne hardly travelled, he corresponded with the eminent of his day.

There are very few people who are not ashamed of having been in love when they no longer love each other.

The mind is always the dupe of the heart.

Nothing is given so profusely as advice.

Usually, we praise only to be praised.

Most people judge men only by their success or their good fortune.

We always like those who admire us; we do not always like those whom we admire.

We rarely find that people have good sense unless they agree with us.

## LA ROCHEFOUCAULD
## 1613-1680

Francois, duc de La Rochefoucauld, was the leading exponent of the maxim. Her used it as a weapon, as a rapier, in fact. It was meant to be swift and shocking, without excuse, palliation or explanation.

One must eat to live, and not live to eat.

## MOLIÈRE
**1622-1673**

Molière was the pseudonym of Jean-Baptiste Poquelin. It might be truer to say that it was his stage name, for he was an actor.

He wrote plays for the public and for the court. Soon, he had his own theatre. It was during a performance of his own play, *La Malade Imaginaire*, that he collapsed on stage and died.

Things are always at their best in their beginning.

Justice without strength is helpless; strength without justice is tyrannical.

We know the truth, not only be reason, but by the heart.

Self is hateful.

We shall die alone.

## BLAISE PASCAL
## 1623-1662

Pascal was a mathematician, physicist, writer and religious philosopher. His life was short but he achieved much.

He invented the first digital calculator. Later he invented the syringe and the hydraulic press. All three served a practical need.

In 1654 he went to live in a convent. Here he pursued scientific research and wrote his *Pénsees*.

In a calm sea, every man is a pilot.

Money begets money.

Blood is thicker than water.

Misery loves company.

## JOHN RAY
## 1627-1705

Ray was a naturalist. The C17 was a period of taxonomy, the listing of objects, plants, and such.

Biological classification owes a great deal to John Ray.

Better one suffer than a nation grieve.

Beware the fury of a patient man.

Jealousy, the jaundice of the soul.

## JOHN DRYDEN
## 1631-1700

Such was Dryden's stature in the C17, that the latter part of that century is known as the Age of Dryden.

In 1688 he was appointed poet laureate. He also wrote plays, both serious and comic. As a playwright he is perhaps best remembered for *All for Love*, while as a poet his verse satire, *Absolom and Achitophel* won general admiration. The latter has lost some of its power because the political arguments of his day, which it satirises, are lost on modern readers.

Dryden's critical essays are important, as also is the influence of his verse and criticism on later generations.

Wherever Law ends, tyranny begins.

A sound mind in a sound body, is a short but full description of a happy state in this world.

## JOHN LOCKE
## 1632-1704

Locke was a philosopher whose main areas of interest were education and politics. He laid the foundations of modern science in terms of science as a body of knowledge.

He maintained, especially in his *Essay Concerning Human Understanding,* that experience is the only true source of knowledge. He was an empiricist.

Our modern ideas of liberal democracy owe much to his essays in 1690, *Two Treatises on Government.* He maintained that a government may justifiably be overthrown if it fails to provide fundamental human rights to its citizens. Thus, he justified the "Glorious Revolution" in England, and provided a philosophical foundation for the American Revolution of 1774 and the French revolution of 1789.

Nature abhors a vacuum.

Man is a social animal.

## BARUCH SPINOZA
## 1632-1677

Spinoza was born in the Netherlands but his family were refugees from Portugal. The family was Jewish.

He himself developed as a rationalist thinker, however, and for this was excommunicated from the Jewish faith. He studied mathematics, linguistics and physics, which were considered to be no-Hebrew subjects.

Spinoza was accused of atheism by Jews and Christians alike, yet there exists in his works a deep spiritual piety. Although he lived in the country and earned a living as a grinder of lenses, he was in communication with the leading minds of his times.

Men are not hanged for stealing horses, but that horses may not be stolen.

## MARQUESS OF HALIFAX
## 1633-1695

George Savile, 1st marquess of Halifax, was a Yorkshireman, and Yorkshiremen are known for being blunt and often controversial. George Savile was neither. He was known as "The Trimmer" from his ability to trim his opinions and actions to suit the government of the day.

After failing to effect a compromise between James 11, a Catholic, and William of Orange, a Protestant, Halifax sides with William and was instrumental in the accession to the throne of William and Mary, ensuring the Protestant succession.

Although widely disliked for his trimming, Halifax understood the need in politics for compromise. He knew that politics, in its active sphere, is not a matter of principles but of what is possible.

Liberality consists less in giving a great deal than in gifts well timed.

Time, which strengthens friendship, weakens love.

There are but three events in a man's life: birth, life and death. He is not conscious of being born, he dies in pain, and he forgets to live.

## LA BRUYÈRE
## 1645-1696

A satirical moralist, La Bruyère wrote what is acknowledged to be a classic of French literature: *Characters or the Manners of this Age*, in 1688.

Although La Bruyère originally studied law, he took a post as a civil servant. Then he went into service with the Condé family, as librarian, and remained with the family for the rest of his life.

He was noted for his biting tongue.

To be always ready for war is the surest way to avoid it.

## FRANÇOIS DE FÉNELON
## 1651-1715

A man of letters and a man of the church. He had what for his time were liberal views on the education of boys and girls.

Fénelon was involved in a controversy over the purpose of mystical prayer. He also believed that Church and State should be separate, so that the Church could, if necessary, criticise the State.

Although he rose to be an archbishop, he fell foul of the Pope in Rome because of his views about prayer. He was effectively exiled to the countryside. It was there, in his later years, that Fénelon composed his maxims.

The end must justify the means.

## MATTHEW PRIOR
## 1664-1721

Matthew Prior was born in Westminster, London, and attended school there. When his father died, and he had to leave the school, his education was financed by a benefactor, the Earl of Dorset.

Prior became a civil servant. He served as secretary to the British ambassador to the Netherlands for several years. He also played an important part in public and secret peace negotiations with France.

He died of cholera and was buried in Westminster Abbey. At his own request, he was buried at the feet of Edmund Spenser, his favourite poet. His own poetry is generally unread today.

Proper words in proper places make the true definition of a style.

## JONATHAN SWIFT
## 1667-1745

Swift is a giant of literature in English.

He was born in Dublin to an expatriate English family. As a boy, he was cared for by an uncle in Ireland.

Swift was a voracious reader, and soon became a writer whose style combined energy and delicacy of style. He became a clergyman, but, like many in his time, this was a source of income rather than a matter of religious fervour.

He became involved in London politics as a controversial author of pamphlets. Later, he found his true strength as a satirist. He gained both popularity and notoriety from his controversial work, which include *A Tale of a Tub* (1704*)*, *A Modest Proposal* (1729), and *Gulliver's Travels* in 1729.

Some praise at morning what they blame at night / But always think the last opinion right.

For fools rush in where angels fear to tread.

What mighty contests rise from trivial things.

## ALEXANDER POPE
## 1688-1744

Like Swift, Alexander Pope is also a giant of literature in English, though his physical stature was that of a dwarf. His health was ruined by a tubercular disease of the spine at the age of twelve years, and he did not grown much thereafter.

While Swift excoriated the human race in prose, Pope used poetry, principally the rhyming couplet. There is no better vehicle for satire than the rhyming couplet and no better practitioner than Pope himself.

A great deal of his work is still read today. While Pope prefers the rapier to the bludgeon, he can also be vicious. Most of the time, however, he combined irony and invective in close harmony. Few escaped his delicate wrath.

A man should be mourned at his birth, not at his death.

Liberty is the right to do what the laws permit.

You have to study a great deal to know a little.

## MONTESQUIEU
## 1689-1755

An outstanding French political philosopher of the C18.

Montesquieu's major work is *The Spirit of Laws*, first published in 1748, after fourteen years of toil.

*The Spirit of Laws* is important because it analyses the relations between political and social structures, between religion and economic development, and other elements that constitute the various forms of society. Montesquieu influenced sociological analysis in both the nineteenth and twentieth centuries.

Whatever is worth doing at all, is worth doing well.

An injury is much sooner forgotten than an insult.

Advice is seldom welcome; and those who want it the most always like it the least.

Wear your learning like your watch, in a private pocket: and do not pull it out and strike it, merely to show that you have one.

Idleness is only the refuge of weak minds.

## EARL OF CHESTERFIELD
## 1694-1773

Philip Dormer Stanhope, 4th Earl of Chesterfield, was a politician, diplomat and wit.

Chesterfield's *Letters to his Son* are a guide to achieving success through good manners and the cultivation of the art of pleasing.  Samuel Johnson them as teaching "the morals of a whore, and the manners of a dancing master."

Love truth, but pardon error.

It is better to risk saving a guilty person than to condemn an innocent one.

The best is the enemy of the good.

History is no more than the portrayal of crimes and misfortunes.

If God did not exist, it would be necessary to invent him.

## VOLTAIRE
## 1694-1778

Voltaire is remembered as a thoroughly decent and witty man. He was not admired in his own country, France, and was even imprisoned in the Bastille on account of his satirical plays. Therefore, he spent much of his life in Switzerland.

He used wit and satire to attack human bigotry and cruelty, and to oppose tyranny. He was always strongly opposed to those who discriminated on the grounds of religious prejudice.

Don't throw stones at your neighbours if your windows are glass.

Where there's marriage without love, there will be love without marriage.

He that lives on hope will die fasting.

The used key is always bright.

There never was a good war or a bad peace.

## BENJAMIN FRANKLIN
## 1706-1790

Franklin was a man of thought and of action. He was a printer and publisher, an author, a diplomat and a revolutionary, and found time also to be a scientist and an inventor. His fine character shines through all his work and his actions.

Franklin helped to draft the Declaration of Independence from Britain, and was a delegate at the negotiations to end the war, which resulted in independence for the thirteen states.

He must have been good company.

The style is the man himself.

Genius is nothing but the greater aptitude for patience.

## GEORGE DE BUFFON
## 1707-1788

Buffon was a French naturalist. His major work, proposed as a series of fifty volumes, consisted of thirty-six at the time of his death.

He was also interested in literature and in writing styles. His *Discourse on Style* may be little read today, except by scholars, but his maxim on style is generally accepted to be true.

He is no wise man that will quit a certainty for an uncertainty.

Knowledge is of two kinds. We know a subject ourselves, or we know where we can find information upon it.

Life is a progress from want to want, not from enjoyment to enjoyment.

It is better to live rich than to die rich.

Whatever you have, spend less.

## SAMUEL JOHNSON
## 1709-1784

It is difficult to know what to say about Johnson that has not been said before. He is a giant of a man, a person to be admired. His views are generally conservative and sensible but Johnson did not often accept the received view of events or of persons.

Johnson was the dominant figure of literary London in the C18. He was not, perhaps, the person as presented by Boswell, but someone infinitely more complex and sympathetic.

In the strict sense of the term, a true democracy has never existed and never will exist.

Provided a man is not mad, he can be cured of every folly but vanity.

## JEAN JACQUES ROUSSEAU
## 1712-1778

Rousseau was born in Geneva, Switzerland, but was very restless, and lived in France, Italy, England and Switzerland. Often, he moved to escape from being incarcerated for debt.

He was argumentative, lacking in social skills, unable to maintain relations with women for very long, and careless of his children's welfare. Yet he also had a good brain that was both enquiring and critical.

In many ways, Rousseau was a prototype Romantic. He is remembered as an influence on the French Revolution of 1789, and on political thinking in Europe in both the nineteenth and twentieth centuries, being a precursor, in many respects, of both communism and fascism,

Man was formed for society.

It is better that ten guilty persons escape than one innocent suffer.

## WILLIAM BLACKSTONE
## 1723-1780

Sir William Blackstone was a judge, a member of parliament, and a university administrator. He is remembered now for his seminal work *Commentaries on the Laws of England*, 1769, which described the state of laws, and became a central text for both British and American universities.

If you have great talents, industry will improve them: if you have but moderate abilities, industry will supply their deficiency.

## SIR JOSHUA REYNOLDS
## 1723-1792

Reynolds was a fine artist who is best remembered as a portrait painter. Few of the eminent of the day escaped his brush, and fewer wished to do so.

He was also a fine writer of prose, and counted eminent literary persons among his closest friends. Boswell's *Life of Johnson* was dedicated to Reynolds. Johnson was painted five times by Reynolds

Reynolds was first president of the Royal Academy.

Silence gives consent.

Measures, not men, have always been my mark.

## OLIVER GOLDSMITH
## 1728-1774

The place of his birth is uncertain but he was educated at Trinity College, Dublin. He presented himself for ordination into the Church of England, was rejected, and studied medicine at Edinburgh, but left without taking a degree.

After wandering in Europe, Goldsmith set up as a physician in London in 1756. He also worked as a teacher. When he applied for a medical post in India he was rejected yet again.

So, like many since, he turned to hack writing. Later, he turned to the writing of plays. As usual, rejection was his reward but in 1773 he gained success with his play *She Stoops to Conquer.*

Johnson concluded that Goldsmith adorned whatever he touched.

The march of the human mind is slow.

All government – indeed, every human benefit and enjoyment, every virtue and every prudent act – is founded on compromise and barter.

Government is a contrivance of human wisdom to provide for human wants.

You can never plan the future by the past.

**EDMUND BURKE**
**1729-1797**

Like Goldsmith, Burke was educated at Trinity College, Dublin. After graduation, he studied law in London. His interests were more on literature and politics than in the law. He made several friends in London, including Samuel Johnson, Reynolds, Goldsmith and the actor-manager David Garrick.

In 1765 Burke was elected as a member of parliament. He brought intellect to the House of Commons. That is rare today.

The principles of a free constitution are irrevocably lost when the legislative power is nominated by the executive.

History is indeed little more than the register of the crimes, follies and misfortunes of mankind.

Corruption, the most infallible symptom of constitutional liberty.

All that is human must retrograde if it does not advance.

## EDWARD GIBBON
## 1737-1794

Gibbon was not much of a man, but he was a great historian.

At Rome in 1763, Gibbon conceived the idea for his great book of the history of the city. "As I sat musing among the ruins of the Capitol, while barefoot friars were singing vespers in the temple of Jupiter, that the idea of writing the decline and fall of the city first started in my mind." Gibbon's style is a complete joy to anyone who cares about the construction of sentences and paragraphs.

The most wasted day of all is that on which we do not laugh.

War to the chateaux, peace to the cottages.

## SEBASTIEN CHAMFORT
## 1741-1794

Born an illegitimate child, Chamfort was raised by a grocer's wife. He received little education but gained notice as a wit. He was taken up by members of pre-revolutionary Paris society.

He became disillusioned, however, and espoused the revolutionary, anti-royalist cause. He became secretary to the Jacobin Club, among the most extreme of groups after the revolution of 1789. After the excesses of the reign of Terror, under Robespierre, Chamfort became more moderate.

Threatened with imprisonment by his political enemies, Chamfort attempted suicide. He died from self-inflicted wounds. Among his sayings is: "Be my brother, or I'll kill you."

Ignorance is preferable to error and he is less remote from the truth who believes nothing than he who believes what is wrong.

Enlighten the people generally, and tyranny and oppression of body and mind will vanish like evil spirits at the dawn of day.

Merchants have no country. The mere spot they stand on does not constitute so strong an attachment as that from which they draw their gains.

## THOMAS JEFFERSON
## 1743-1826

Some people seem completely admirable, despite human foibles, of which no person is free. Among the admirable in the Eighteenth century are Samuel Johnson and Benjamin Franklin. To that number must be added the name of Thomas Jefferson, chief author of the Declaration of Independence, and successively governor of the state of Virginia, ambassador to Paris, secretary of state (foreign secretary), vice-president, and from 1801-09 the third president of the United States.

The sleep of reason produces monsters.

## FRANCISCO JOSÉ DE GOYA
## 1746-1828

Goya was first a bullfighter and then a painter.

He painted the portraits of four kings of Spain.

*The Disasters of War* depicts scenes from the French invasion of Spain from 1810-14.

Goya's last paintings, showing cruelty and terror, with human faces distorted, indicate a man who is becoming mad.

Art is long, life short; judgement difficult, opportunity transient.

Life teaches us to be less harsh with ourselves and with others.

Doubt grows with knowledge.

First and last, what is demanded of genius is love of truth.

## JOHANN Von GOETHE
## 1749-1832

When Goethe was born, Germany was a group of large and often disparate states. Goethe spent most of his life at the court of the Duke of Weimar. He held many positions, and was finally raised to the peerage. He excelled at drama and the novel. Much of his work was autobiographical or confessional, not least *The Sorrows of Young Werther*, published in 1774, and the series of novels known as the *Wilhelm Meister* series.

Goethe's work was made popular in English by being translated by Thomas Carlyle.

Nature is not a cause but a result.

The more terrible God appears to us, the more our prayers must become ardent.

## JOSEPH DE MAISTRE
## 1753-1821

De Maistre was a deeply conservative moralist. He spent most of his adult life in exile, because of the invasions of the Italian states by Napoleon. He spent fourteen years in Russia, as envoy from the King of Sardinia. Later, he served as a minister to the King of Sardinia.

De Maistre believed in autocratic rule by kings and popes. He was opposed to science and to liberal notions. In short, he was completely at odds with everyone except the King of Sardinia and the Pope. For him the true guardian of social order was the public executioner. Given his political premises, his thinking was always logical. He was a man born out of his time, fruitlessly trying to stem the changes within society. The notions of the French revolutionaries are remembered; de Maistre is little remembered.

The joke loses everything when the joker laughs himself.

Whatever is not forbidden, is permitted.

Life is only error
And death is knowledge.

Against stupidity the very gods themselves contend in vain.


## JOHANN von SCHILLER
## 1759-1805

A German dramatist and poet, Schiller was central to that period of German literary history known as *Sturm und Drang* - Storm and Stress.

This was part of the Romantic Movement, its members being inspired by Rousseau and the desire to return to nature and natural education. Herder and Goethe were also involved in what Margaret Drabble has called "a period of literary ferment."

Population, when unchecked, increases in a geometrical ratio. Subsistence only increases in an arithmetical ratio.

## THOMAS ROBERT MALTHUS
## 1766-1834

Although a cleric in the Church of England, Malthus held views on population control that would not endear him to Christians today.

Malthus was an economist and a pessimist. Human hope for happiness is a vain pursuit. Population growth, unless checked, will outrun production. Population will be controlled by famine, plague and ill health.

He published many tracts and pamphlets on economy, but none received the wide notice of his *Essay on the Principle of Population*, first published in 1798, and revised and lengthened in 1803.

The only thing I am afraid of is fear.

My rule always was to do the business of the day in the day.

Nothing except a battle lost can be half so melancholy as a battle won.

## DUKE OF WELLINGTON
## 1769-1852

Arthur Wellesley, 1st Duke of Wellington, is for many people Britain's greatest general, higher in stature than even Cromwell or Marlborough. Wellington never lost a battle. He fought many battles in India and afterwards expelled the French from Spain in 1814, after many arduous years. He defeated Napoleon at two battles in 1815, Quatre-Bras and Waterloo.

He was Prime Minister of the United Kingdom from 1828 to 1830. He subsequently held other cabinet posts until 1846.

Wellington was a conservative who always thought and spoke reasonably. He was a lover of many beautiful women.

The history of the world is none other than the progress of the consciousness of freedom.

What experience and history teach is this – that people and governments never have learned anything from history, or acted on principles deduced from it.

## G W F HEGEL
## 1770-1831

Georg Wilhelm Friedrich Hegel was one of the world's most influential philosophers. He was one of the makers of the nineteenth and twentieth centuries.

His work is difficult to understand by the layman. In brief, he held that mind and nature (consciousness and external objects) are part of one whole. Development takes place through contradictions being resolved in a unity. This he termed the "dialectic". The task of philosophers is to understand the rationality of what exists.

Hegel was a conservative. Nevertheless, he was a powerful influence on people of the left, such as Karl Marx and Friedrich Engels.

Men are we and must grieve when even the shade
Of that which once was great has passed away.

Strongest minds
Are often those of whom the noisy world
Hears least.

Minds which have nothing to confer
Find little to perceive.

Action is transitory, -a step, a blow,
The motion of a muscle, this way or that –
'Tis done, and in the after-vacancy
We wonder at ourselves like men betrayed.
Suffering is permanent, obscure and dark,
And shares the nature of infinity.

## WILLIAM WORDSWORTH
## 1770-1850

Wordsworth was one of the group known as the Lake Poets but his influence has extended all over the Anglophone world.

He started out in adult life as a radical, influenced by Rousseau and the French revolution of 1789, but gradually became a conservative in politics.

Avoid shame, but do not seek glory – nothing so expensive as glory.

Live always in the best company when you read.

Never give way to melancholy; resist in steadily, for the habit will encroach.

## SIDNEY SMITH
## 1771-1845

Having one of the world's most common surnames cannot be easy for a person anxious to make his mark in the literary world. Yet Sidney Smith came to be known as the Smith of Smiths.

He was liberal in politics, humane in his dealings, and renowned for his great wit. He spent most of his life as a parson with rural churches but was active in literary and political circles in both Edinburgh and London.

The human species is, according to the best theory I can form of it, composed of two distinct races, the men who borrow, and the men who lend.

The good things of life are not to be had singly, but come to us with a mixture.

## CHARLES LAMB
## 1775-1834

Few people impress with their innate goodness. One is Charles Lamb. The tenderness with which he cared for his mad sister Mary – who had stabbed their mother to death – attests to his goodness.

He is remembered chiefly for his summaries of Shakespeare's plays, *Lamb's Tales from Shakespeare,* and for pleasant and diverting essays. He was very keen on the playing cards, especially whist.

To marry is to halve your rights and double your duties.

Hatred comes from the heart; contempt from the head; and neither feeling is quite within our control.

There is no more mistaken path to happiness than worldliness, revelry, high life.

Do not shorten the morning by getting up late; look upon it as the quintessence of life, as to a certain extent sacred.

## ARTHUR SCHOPENHAUER
## 1788-1860

Schopenhauer was a German philosopher. He was deeply pessimistic. The material world, he believed, was an illusion and our only contact with any kind of reality is in our Will, our consciousness of being an individual self.

The notions of God, free will and the hope of immortality after death are all illusions.

There is nothing so captivating as new knowledge.

Truth in all its kinds is most difficult to win; and truth in medicine is the most difficult of all.

Beware of language for it is often a great cheat.

We should always presume the disease to be curable, until its own nature prove it otherwise.

## PETER M LATHAM
## 1789-1875

(The Editors have failed to find biographical details of Latham, but they cannot claim to have made a conscientious or scholarly search. Latham was probably an American. It is likely that he was a physician.

Information from readers would be welcomed. Such information will be included in revised editions of this book, and duly acknowledged.)

A well-written Life is almost as rare as a well-spent one.

A poet without love were a physical and metaphysical impossibility.

Man is a tool-using animal. Without tools he is nothing, with tools he is all.

All that mankind has done, thought, gained or been: it is lying as in magic preservation in the pages of books.

The history of the world is but the biography of great men.

**THOMAS CARLYLE**
**1795-1881**

Carlyle did a great deal to introduce German literature to Britain, not least the leading members of the *Sturm und Drang* movement.

His voluminous correspondence with his wife, Jane, to whom he wrote daily even when they were under the same roof, is likely to be his legacy, but even here it is Jane who emerges as the person to admire, with her controlled and accessible writing style.

What is the first part of politics? Education. The second? Education. And the third? Education.

## JULES MICHELET
## 1798-1874

Michelet is one of the world's major historians. He was keeper of the National Historical Archives of France for twenty-one years. His major work is his history of France, in seventeen volumes written over twenty-four years. There was a break in the middle when Michelet wrote his seven-volume history of the French Revolution.

Michelet wanted to discover a science of historical writing. He wanted to mix history with philosophy.

A good introduction to Michelet, and the effects on him of reading Vico - an Italian philosopher of history as a cyclical phenomenon – can be found in the first sixty pages of *To the Finland Station* by Edmund Wilson.

There is a knowledge which is desirable, though nothing come of it, as being of itself a treasure, and a sufficient remuneration of years of labour.

A great, memory does not make a philosopher, any more than a dictionary can be called a grammar

## JOHN HENRY NEWMAN
## 1801-1890

Newman was an influential figure in Victorian England. Ordained into the Church of England, he moved steadily toward the Roman Catholic Church, and took many others with him.

His life was one of celibacy and almost monastic abstinence from the world, but he was a writer of vigour and style. His ideas on education were influential.

He is remembered as a writer of popular hymns, of the poem *The Dream of Gerontius* (set to music by Sir Edward Elgar) and of *Apologia Pro Vita Sua,* a defence of his life and opinions which he wrote after a strong attack by Charles Kingsley.

An invasion of armies can be resisted but not an idea whose time has come.

The supreme happiness of life is the conviction that we are loved.

Great blunders are often made, like large ropes, of a multitude of fibres.

No one ever keeps a secret so well as a child.

Social prosperity means man happy, the citizen free, the nation great.

Thought is the labour of the intellect, reverie is its pleasure.

## VICTOR HUGO
## 1802-1885

Poet, dramatist and novelist, Victor-Marie Hugo was a leader of the Romantic Movement in France.

Hugo is chiefly remembered today for two novels: *Notre Dame de Paris* (1831) and *Les Miserables* (1862).

A good heart is better than all the heads in the world.

The easiest person to deceive is one's own self.

## EDWARD BULWER-LYTTON
## 1803-1873

Bulwer-Lytton was a politician. He lived in style and felt it necessary to earn money from writing plays and novels. He was always fashionable and never willingly or knowingly opposed public reading tastes.

Among the works that are still read and enjoyed are *The Last days of Pompeii* and *Rienzi.*

Edward George Earle Bulwer-Lytton is often confused with Edward Robert Bulwer-Lytton, 1st Earl of Lytton. They were, respectively, father and son. It was the father who began a novel, "It was a dark and stormy night."

To be great is to be misunderstood.

Nothing can bring you peace but yourself.

The only reward of virtue is virtue; the only way to have a friend is to be one.

Nothing astonishes me so much as common sense and plain dealing.

Life is not so short but that there is always time enough for courtesy.

## RALPH WALDO EMERSON
## 1803-1882

Emerson was born in Boston, Massachusetts. After his university education became a Unitarian minister but soon resigned and travelled in Europe, where he met, among many, Wordsworth, Coleridge and Carlyle.

He was a philosopher, poet and essayist. He praised the virtues of hard work and self-reliance.

What we anticipate seldom occurs; what we least expected generally happens.

Youth is a blunder; manhood a struggle; old age a regret.

Everything comes if a man will only wait.

Increased means and increased leisure are the two civilisers of man.

Everyone likes flattery; and when you come to Royalty you should lay it on with a trowel.


## BENJAMIN DISRAELI
## 1804-1881

Disraeli was of Jewish family origin but was baptised into the Church of England. He started his working life in a solicitor's office and wrote novels. In 1837 he was elected to parliament but only after four unsuccessful attempts. He was derided as a dandy because of his dress, as a foreigner because of his appearance, and as an adventurer because of his wit.

Disraeli was the true founder of the modern Conservative Party.

There is only one happiness in life, to love and be loved.

The whole secret of the study of nature lies in learning how to use one's eyes.

## GEORGE SAND
## 1804-1876

George Sand was a woman who dressed as a man, often walked like a man, and smoked cigars. Yet she was always a woman. She had sexual liaisons with most of the leading writers of her day in France but is chiefly remembered today for her affair with Frederic Chopin.

Sand's Romantic novels are probably little read today. Still read, however, is her account of *A Winter in Majorca*, where she went with Chopin and her two children.

In later life, George Sand became quite respectable and matronly, and more conservative in politics. This is often the case with youthful rebels, once they have made their mark. Yet she was, in several ways, the first feminist, and deserves to be remembered for that.

Whatever crushes individuality is despotism, by whatever name it may be called.

Everyone who receives the protection of society owes a return for the benefit.

It is better to be Socrates dissatisfied than a pig satisfied.

## JOHN STUART MILL
## 1806-1873

Mill was a child prodigy and a polymath. His father, James Mill, was an economist, historian and philosopher, who was determined that his first son should become a leader of men. Thus, John Stuart was studying Greek at the age of three years and by eight was studying Latin, logic, mathematics and political economy. His father was nothing if not rigorous.

After university, Mill spent thirty-five years in the service of the East India Company.

Mill was a voracious reader and writer. He came to believe that progress and amelioration would come not from a single system, but by the tolerance by society of diverse opinions.

The highest possible stage in moral culture is when we recognise that we ought to control our thoughts.

Progress has been much more general than retrogression.

From the war of nature, from famine and death, the production of the higher animals directly follows.

## CHARLES DARWIN
## 1809-1882

It is difficult not to admire Darwin. He is now rightly remembered as the main, though by no means the only, figure in propounding the theory of evolution by natural selection.

His journal, written while a member of the crew of *HMS Beagle*, from 1831 to 1836, is a pleasure to read. In *On the Origin of Species*, 1859, Darwin assembles a vast amount of evidence for evolution as a process.

He did not seek public notice. He did not attempt to amass wealth. But he turned the world upside down.

Drink! for, once dead, you shall never return.

## EDWARD FITZGERALD
## 1809-1883

Fitzgerald was a translator of note, translating plays from Spanish and Greek. He published a collection of aphorisms and wrote critical accounts of the poetry of Crabbe. His friends were among the most eminent in literary society, and included Tennyson and Carlyle.

Yet Fitzgerald is remembered today chiefly as the translator of *The Rubáiyát of Omar Khayyam,* published in 1859, the same year as Darwin shook the world with his theory of evolution. Fitzgerald's work was no less revolutionary, in that it praised the virtues of the life of an epicure in what was still a staid Christian society.

Fitzgerald was often very lonely and melancholy, which may in part have been the need to conceal his homosexual preferences.

Selfishness is the greatest curse of the human race.

## WILLIAM GLADSTONE
## 1809-1898

Gladstone was a British liberal politician. He towered like a colossus over the second part of the nineteenth century. He was returned to, power as prime minister for an unrivalled four times.

Gladstone had great energy, well into old age. As well as writing and making speeches, leading the government, speaking often in the House of Commons, making speeches throughout the country, and keeping a voluminous diary, he wrote widely on matters to do with the church.

To some he is the epitome of liberal good work, with a zeal for reform. To as many more, he appears as a sanctimonious old bore.

Truth is generally the best vindication against slander.

## ABRAHAM LINCOLN
## 1809-1865

Lincoln failed in just about everything he turned his hand to, until finally he achieved the presidency of the United States. Even then, he won only because of splits over states' rights and the issue of slavery.

Lincoln was a complex man and yet also a simple man. His chief aims were to prevent the secession from the Union of the southern states, and to prevent the spread of slavery to the newer states and territories to the west.

To achieve this, he prosecuted war against the secessionist southern confederate states, and won. Elected for a second term, Lincoln was shot dead by John Booth Wilkes while attending the theatre in Washington.

Lincoln is perhaps the best loved of American presidents and the one most deserving of that love. Her was that strange phenomenon: an honest man in politics.

Property is theft.

## PIERRE JOSEPH PROUDHON
## 1809-1865

Proudhon is a man easy to admire and difficult to agree with.

He was a libertarian socialist and in many ways the father of anarchism as a political philosophy.

He came from a poor peasant family and was a worker all his life. In 1848 he was elected to the new assembly but was soon imprisoned for criticising the president, Louis Bonaparte, who was soon to seize power as Emperor Napoleon the Third.

From 1858 to 1862, Proudhon was in exile in Belgium. After receiving a pardon, he returned to France and continued the struggle. He died comparatively young, partly because of the strain of overwork.

It is impossible to reduce human society to one level.

## POPE LEO XIII
## 1810-1903

Leo was pope from 1878 to 1903. This was not an easy time to be pope, because of the many assaults, frontal and oblique, against traditional Christian and other religious belief.

He had to respond to sophisticated scientific research in many areas, and to the widespread acceptance of the theories concerning evolution from Darwin, Herbert Spencer and others. In addition, there were political forces such as Socialism, Liberalism and nascent Fascism.

Leo's encyclical of 1891, *Rerum Novarum*, of New Things, sought to confront the changes in a way that combined traditional beliefs with common sense. He emphasised the need for social justice, not least the rights of workers to be treated better. In this way, Leo hoped to stem the tide of political change. It was a fruitless attempt.

Observation is a passive science, experimentation an active science.

Science increases our power in proportion as it lowers our pride.

Man can learn nothing unless he proceeds from the known to the unknown.

We must never make experiments to confirm our ideas, but simply to control them.

## CLAUDE BERNARD
## 1813-1878

Bernard was a French physiologist. He showed that digestion of food takes place along the whole intestine and not only in the stomach. He was also the first to demonstrate the functions of the pancreas regarding digestion, several functions of the liver, and the control of body temperature.

Life can only be understood backwards; but it must be lived forwards.

It requires moral courage to grieve; it requires religious courage to rejoice.

## SÖREN KIERKEGAARD
## 1813-1855

A Danish philosopher, Kierkegaard is considered to be the founder of Existentialism, a view of life that had considerable influence on literature and politics in the twentieth century.

Kierkegaard was a committed Christian. He disagreed with much that Hegel wrote and stated that reason cannot prove certain beliefs, but only a great leap, an act of faith. Subjective commitment was important.

He was often ill and in pain, and died young.

I think that we must be men first and subjects afterwards.

Beware of all enterprises that require new clothes.

The man who goes alone can start today; but he who travels with another must wait till that other is ready.

There is no odour so bad as that which arises from goodness tainted.

A man is rich in proportion to the number of things he can afford to let alone.

## HENRY DAVID THOREAU
## 1817-1862

Thoreau worked at different times as a teacher, private tutor, surveyor and maker of pencils.

*Walden, or Life in the Woods*, (1854) describes two years when Thoreau lived alone in a wooden hut by the side of a lake, and attempted to be self-sufficient. Though little noticed at the time, the book has since won general acceptance as a classic of American writing.

The ruling ideas of each age have ever been the ruling ideas of its ruling class.

## KARL MARX      1818-1883
## FRIEDRICH ENGELS  1820-1895

Some pairs seem to go together, like Laurel and Hardy. Marx without Engels would seem almost impossible.

Much has been written about Marx and Marxism, though less about Engels. Only recently has it been shown that Engels had a greater influence than is sometimes accepted on the development of socialist ideas.

Engels was the son of a rich German cotton manufacturer, and was sent to England to tend the family's factories on Manchester. This was how he first met Karl Marx. Engels gave money and time to Marx, who was in many ways a sponger.

Engels was very much a human being. He enjoyed riding with the hounds, and liked girls from the working classes.

A wise scepticism is the first attribute of a good critic.

## JAMES RUSSELL LOWELL
## 1819-1891

An academic, literary critic, and editor of the influential *Atlantic Monthly*, Lowell was also a poet and essayist.

He was part of an established family in Massachusetts, and was thus educated at Harvard University.

To know anything well involves a profound sensation of ignorance.

The essence of lying is in deception, not in words.

There is no wealth but life.

There is no law of history any more than of a kaleidoscope.

Life without industry is guilt; industry without art is brutality.

## JOHN RUSKIN
## 1819-1900

Even one hundred years after his death, Ruskin continues to divide. In his own time he was extremely important as a critic, both in the arts and in political matters. He was a conservative who had a great influence over socialists and working people. A college in Oxford is named after Ruskin.

In many ways he never developed sexually or socially. Yet he wrote like an angel.

The mind of man may be compared to a musical instrument with a certain range of notes, beyond which in both directions we have an infinitude of silence.

The brightest flashes in the world of thought are incomplete until they have been proved to have their counterparts in the world of facts.

It is as fatal as it is cowardly to blink facts because they are not to our taste.

Superstition may be defined as constructive religion which has grown incongruous with intelligence.

## JOHN TYNDALL
## 1820-1893

John Tyndall was a populariser of science from his position as professor at the British Institute. He had many friends in scientific and literary circles, including Charles Darwin, Herbert Spencer and Leslie Stephen.

Tyndall is also remembered as the discoverer of the Tyndall Effect.

Progress is not an accident, but a necessity.

Opinion is ultimately determined by the feelings, and not by the intellect.

Every cause produces more than one effect.

## HERBERT SPENCER
## 1820-1903

Spencer was a sociologist, psychologist (when these were new disciplines) and a philosopher. He sought to write in depth about most subjects. His aim was to achieve a synthesis of all knowledge by extending Darwin's theories of evolution to all fields of human endeavour.

He was very popular in both Britain and the United States. He was a close friend of Marian Evans, also known as George Eliot the novelist.

It was Spencer, not Darwin, who said that evolution is "the survival of the fittest," and he was not speaking only of physical fitness. He also first claimed that proficiency at billiards is the sign of a misspent youth. Spencer's own youth was largely misspent.

The only medicine for suffering, crime, and all the other woes of mankind, is wisdom.

There is the greatest practical benefit in making a few failures early in life.

Size is not grandeur and territory does not make a nation.

Irrationally held truths may be more harmful than reasoned errors.

## THOMAS HENRY HUXLEY
## 1825-1895

Huxley studied medicine at London University. He spent some time at sea as a ship's surgeon. Later, he delivered lectures and wrote books and essays, mainly on science and religion.

Thomas Huxley is chiefly remembered as a vigorous populariser of Darwin's work and theories.

He coined the word "agnostic" for someone who has an open mind on matters of religious belief. Huxley was a great believer in open minds and scientific enquiry.

One of the greatest pains to human nature is the pain of a new idea.

It is good to be without vices, but it is not good to be without temptations.

## WALTER BAGEHOT
## 1826-1877

Bagehot was a political commentator, an economist and a literary critic. It is as a political thinker that he is chiefly studied today.

He was editor of *The Economist* for seventeen years and his great work is *The English Constitution*, published in 1867. This book is worthy of study, especially at a time when many people seem intent on destroying the English constitution, which has been hard-won over a thousand years.

Nobody, including the present editors, ever seems quite sure how to pronounce Walter's surname.

All happy families resemble each other, each unhappy family is unhappy in its own way.

Pure and complete sorrow is as impossible as pure and complete joy.

The strongest of all warriors are these two – Time and Patience.

The more is given, the less people will work for themselves, and the less they work the more their poverty will increase.

## LEO TOLSTOY
## 1828-1910

Tolstoy was born into a Russian noble family and as a young man he fought in the Crimean War. From this experience there came *Tales from Sebastopol*, 1856. Later, he wrote *War and Peace*, set in the times of the Napoleonic Wars, and *Anna Karenina*, the story of a passionate married woman falling in love with a young army officer, and the tragic consequences of their illicit romance.

Tolstoy was a fraud, able to deceive himself and others.

Power tends to corrupt and absolute power corrupts absolutely.

Liberty is not a means to a higher political end. It is itself the highest political end.

Truth is the only merit that gives dignity and worth to history.

## LORD ACTON
## 1834-1902

Acton has been called the greatest historian who never wrote a book of history. He is remembered, however, as the man who, while professor of history, coordinated the work on the important Cambridge Modern History series.

He was a catholic but he clashed with the papacy over liberalism. Acton was a liberal in politics and religion. He was a close friend of Gladstone, who elevated him to the peerage.

His essays are still a delight to read, in spite of a rather heavy Victorian moral stance.

A round man cannot be expected to fit in a square hole right away. He must have time to modify his shape.

Grief can take care of itself, but to get the full value of a joy you must have somebody to divide it with.

Man is the only animal that blushes. Or needs to.

Pity is for the living, envy is for the dead.

## MARK TWAIN
## 1835-1910

Born into a poor southern family, he was raised in Hannibal, Missouri. Here he lived the material that was to become *The Adventures of Tom Sawyer* and *the Adventures of Huckleberry Finn.*

He was born on the day that Halley's comet could be observed, and died on the very day, seventy-five years later, when the comet returned.

All experience is an arch, to build upon.

Practical politics consists in ignoring facts.

## HENRY BROOKS ADAMS
## 1838-1918

Adams was an historian and a man of letters but is remembered as the author of one of the very best autobiographies ever written in English. This was *The Education of Henry Adams.*

This autobiography remains readable and interesting.

Evolution is not a force but a process; not a cause but a law.

You cannot demonstrate an emotion or prove an aspiration.

It s not enough to do good; one must do it in the right way.

The great business of life is to be, to do, to do without, and to depart.

## JOHN MORLEY
## 1838-1923

Morley was a liberal politician and a follower of Gladstone, whose biography he wrote.

He was a prolific essayist but his style adorns all he writes. This is not common among politicians and journalists. It is the style, rather than the content, that maintains his interest even today, nearly eight decades after his death.

Life is an end in itself, and the only question as to whether it is worth living, is whether you have enough of it.

Life, not the parson, teaches conduct.

The life of the law has not been logic: it has been experience.

## OLIVER WENDELL HOLMES
## 1841-1935

Holmes was born before Henry Morton Stanley, Gerard Manley Hopkins and Oscar Wilde, yet lived long enough to advise President Franklin Delano Roosevelt. Among the wisest judges produced in the United States, or anywhere else, for that matter.

A thing is important if anyone thinks it is important.

Genius means little more than the faculty of perceiving in an unhabitual way.

The moral flabbiness born of the exclusive worship of the bitch-goddess success. That – with the squalid cash interpretation put on the word success – is our national disease.

## WILLIAM JAMES
## 1842-1910

A psychologist, and brother of Henry James the novelist, William James wrote an important book on the psychology of religion and religious conversion under the title *Varieties of Religious Experience*. It remains in print and remains worth reading.

Mutual aid is as much a law of animal life as mutual struggle.

## PETER KROPOTKIN
## 1842-1921

Peter Alexeivich Kropotkin came from a noble family yet became an anarchist dedicated to the destruction of nobility, rank, class, and indeed all coercion.

He was a geographer but from 1870 until his death in 1921, he was leader of the European anarchist movement. As well as geographer and politician, Kropotkin was a zoologist, historian and sociologist. He believed that mutual aid, rather than constant struggle, was the basis for evolution. This brought him into conflict with Darwinists.

Kropotkin was opposed to all forms of government that were authoritarian. When he died in 1921, thousands attended his funeral. Yet the communists under Lenin were already stifling all opposition.

All historical books which contain no lies are extremely tedious.

Man is so made that he can find relaxation from one kind of labour only by taking up another.

A good critic is one who tells of his mind's adventures among masterpieces.

Lovers who love truly do not write down their happiness.

A tale without love is like beef without mustard.

## ANATOLE FRANCE
## 1844-1924

Jean-Anatole-Francois Thibault was a French novelist who used the pseudonym of Anatole France. His novels are dominated by social satire.

In 1921 he was awarded the Nobel Prize for literature, but he is not much read or noticed today.

Distrust all in whom the impulse to punish is powerful.

It is not the strength but the duration of great sentiments that makes great men.

All prejudices may be traced back to the intestines.

## FRIEDRICH NIETZSCHE
## 1844-1900

Friedrich Nietzsche must be one of the most misunderstood men in politics and literature.

His ideas are not always clear but it is certain that he rejected Christianity and Christian moral teachings. He believed that Christianity was the response of slaves.

Nietzsche has been called the father of Nazism, because certain Nazi leaders took over his ideas about the Superman. In fact, Nietzsche rejected all forms of nationalism and doctrines of political power based on authoritarianism.

His star has risen in the past thirty years.

Marriage is like life in this – that it is a field of battle and not a bed of roses.

There is no duty we so much underrate as the duty of being happy.

To travel hopefully is a better thing than to arrive.

## ROBERT LOUIS STEVENSON
### 1850-1894

Best known as a writer of books for children – *Treasure Island* and *Kidnapped*, for example – Stevenson's range was very wide. He collaborated on plays, wrote historical novels, edited a famous book of poetry, and was a prolific journalist. In addition , he was a fine and provocative essayist.

Because Stevenson suffered from tuberculosis, he travelled a great deal in search of a good climate. This resulted in interesting travel books but not in good health. *Travels with a Donkey* is still worth reading.

Stevenson died in Samoa from brain haemorrhage.

There is no sin except stupidity.

There is no such thing as a moral or immoral book. Books are well written, or badly written. That is all.

A man cannot be too careful in the choice of his enemies.

Experience is the name everyone gives to their mistakes.

Charity creates a multitude of sins.

As long as war is regarded as wicked, it will always have its fascination. When it is looked upon as vulgar, it will cease to be popular.


**OSCAR WILDE**
**1854-1900**

It is for the wit of his plays that Wilde is chiefly remembered. He was among the finest writers of paradox in English. Wilde's private life was a mess. His work is pure genius.

Being entirely honest with oneself is a good exercise.

The psychic development of the individual is a short repetition of the course of development of the race.

Analogies prove nothing, that is quite true, but they can make one feel more at home.

Religion is an illusion and it derives its strength from the fact that it falls in with our instinctual desires.

## SIGMUND FREUD
## 1856-1939

Freud is the recognised father of psycho-analysis. Among his many insights and contributions to the field of health are the recognition of childhood sexuality and the workings of the unconscious mind.

Freud rejected religion, claiming it to be an illusion based on fear of death and annihilation of the body.

The golden rule is that there is no golden rule.

He who can, does. He who cannot, teaches.

Marriage is popular because it combines the maximum of temptation with the maximum of opportunity.

Lack of money is the root of all evil.

## GEORGE BERNARD SHAW
## 1856-1950

Shaw was born in Ireland. He was a music critic of great knowledge and perception. He also wrote novels of little value. It was as a dramatist that he found fame, and later as a wit and controversialist.

Shaw talked too much and wrote too much. In later life he made a complete ass of himself by supporting dictators such as Stalin in Russia, Mussolini in Italy and Hitler in Germany. Since his death, his stock has declined. Few of his plays are revived, and his other work is largely neglected. There is no good reason why his stock should appreciate in future.

You shall judge of a man by his foes as well as by his friends.

Vanity plays lurid tricks with our memory.

We live, as we dream – alone.

The mind of man is capable of anything – because everything is in it, all the past as well as all the future.

**JOSEPH CONRAD**
**1857-1924**

Jozef Teodor Konrad Korzeniowski came from a Polish family with noble connections.

As a young man, Jozef joined the French mercantile marine and then the British merchant service. He rose to be skipper of various boats. He went to many parts of the world, most notably the East. He also became captain of a river steamer in the Congo. This journey was the basis for *The Heart of Darkness.*

He is supreme in writing of the sea.

No man is justified in doing evil on the ground of expediency.

Speak softly and carry a big stick; you will go far.

## THEODORE ROOSEVELT
## 1858-1918

Roosevelt became president by accident. He was vice-president when McKinley was assassinated in 1901. He served as president until 1909. An attempt to run for the presidency in 1912 as an independent resulted in defeat by Woodrow Wilson.

Theodore Roosevelt was very much a maverick in politics. He led a commando group known as the rough riders in Cuba during the Spanish-American war of 1898. After 1914 he advocated US entry into the First World War, which happened in 1917.

He won the Nobel Prize for Peace in 1906 for helping to end the Russo-Japanese War, and he is one of the presidents whose features are carved in Mount Rushmore. Teddy bears are named after him.

Rationalism is an adventure in the clarification of thought.

There are no whole truths; all truths are half truths.

The fact of the instability of evil is the moral order of the world.

**ALFRED NORTH WHITEHEAD**
**1861-1947**

Whitehead was a professor of mathematics and later of philosophy. He collaborated with Bertrand Russell on works of mathematics and philosophy.

He was well known in both Britain and the United States. Today, he is little read and hardly noted. His happens to some notable people: after their death, they are quickly forgotten.

Those who cannot remember the past are condemned to repeat it.

The highest form of vanity is love of fame. There is no cure for birth and death save to enjoy the interval.

The young man who has not wept is a savage, and the old man who will not laugh is a fool.

## GEORGE SANTAYANA
## 1863-1952

Santayana was born in to a Spanish family in Boston, Massachusetts. He was educated in the United States. After 1912 he spent most of his time in Europe, mainly in France and Britain, though he died in Italy.

George Santayana was a speculative philosopher. He believed that ideas existed on a higher plane than material things such as the body.

He is worth reading for his fine prose style, though sometimes he rather overdoes his effects. One puts down his books with the feeling that here was a happy man.

If a poet interprets a poem of his own, he limits its suggestibility.

Only two topics can be of the least interest to a serious and studious mood (mind?) – sex and the dead.

In life courtesy and self-possession, and in the arts style, are the sensible impressions of the free mind.

## W B YEATS
## 1865-1939

As a man, William Butler Yeats often appears confused and inadequate. His political opinions varied between leftist revolution and admiration for fascism. He believed in fairies and various aspects of the occult. His relations with women were rarely successful on a sexual level.

As a poet, however, he is sublime, one of the greatest poets who have ever written in English.

Mathematics, rightly viewed, possesses not only truth, but supreme beauty.

It is preoccupation with possessions, more than anything else, that prevents men from living freely and nobly.

To fear love is to fear life, and those who fear life are already three parts dead.

## BERTRAND RUSSELL
## 1872-1970

Bertrand Russell, the third Earl, was the grandson of a famous prime minister of Britain. He was a pioneer in mathematical logic and philosophy, and an acute observer and participant in politics.

In the First World War he was a pacifist and went to prison for writing pacifist articles. As an old man he went to prison again, for organising resistance to atomic weapons.

His *A History of Western Philosophy*, written after World War 11, was both popular and influential.

All slang is metaphor, and all metaphor is poetry.

A good novel tells us the truth about its hero, but a bad novel tells us the truth about its author.

Poets do not go mad; but chess players do.

If a thing is worth doing, it is worth doing badly.

Happiness is a mystery, like religion, and should never be rationalised.


## G K CHESTERTON
## 1874-1936

Born in London, Gilbert Keith Chesterton was a novelist (*The Napoleon of Notting Hill*), poet (*The Donkey; The Battle of Lepanto*), a writer of short stories, a writer of detective fiction (The Father Brown Stories), a literary critic, an essayist, mainly on religious and social themes, and a prolific journalist.

Chesterton is a master of paradox. He liked English beer and the English countryside.

The maxim of the British people is "Business as usual."

There is no finer investment for any community than putting milk into babies.

Those who can win a war well can rarely make a good peace and those who could make a good peace would never have won the war.

## WINSTON CHURCHILL
## 1874-1965

It is difficult to say anything about Winston Churchill that has not been said or written before.

He was a politician all his life. His policies and enthusiasms were often foolish. He was dedicated to the construction of his own legend.

He was, when all is said and done, a great commoner and in 1940 the saviour of his country from German invasion and Nazi tyranny.

There are women who are not beautiful but only look that way.

An aphorism is never exactly truthful. It is either a half-truth or a truth and a half.

**KARL KRAUS**
**1874-1936**

Kraus was an Austrian man of letters. He condemned the First World War as the destroyer of all that was best in the European literary tradition.

He is chiefly remembered today as an aphorist.

Where love rules, there is no will to power; and where power predominates, there love is lacking.

The meeting of two personalities is like the contact of two chemical substances: if there is any reaction, both are transformed.

## CARL GUSTAV JUNG
## 1875-1961

Jung was a Swiss psychiatrist who collaborated with Freud on the development of psycho-analytical theory until the two men quarrelled.

Jung became more interested in the occult, and in race memories. He introduced the terms: extrovert/introvert; archetype; complex; collective unconscious and individuation.

His work is in many ways more interesting than Freud's, but just as unscientific and misguided.

The most beautiful thing we can experience is the mysterious. It is the source of all true art and science.

The whole of science is nothing more than a refinement of everyday thinking.

I shall never believe that God plays dice with the universe.

$E = mc2$

## ALBERT EINSTEIN
## 1879-1955

Albert Einstein was a German-Swiss physicist responsible for the formulation of the theories of relativity. He was awarded the Nobel Prize for Physics in 1921.

Einstein was deprived of his position by the Nazis in 1933, because he was of Jewish family origin. He migrated to the United States, where his theories were influential in the development of atomic physics and ultimately of atomic bombs.

He is a man to excite admiration.

The history of liberty has largely been the history of the observance of procedural safeguards.

## FELIX FRANKFURTER
## 1882-1965

A noted American scholar and judge of the Supreme Court, Frankfurter was born in Vienna and did not settle in the United States until he was twelve years old.

His judgements are important because they confront the question of the integrity of government and the rights of individuals. Frankfurter was wise enough to recognise that individual freedom must sometimes be sacrificed. Nevertheless, he overturned a requirement that children, including Jehovah's Witnesses, should have to salute the American flag.

War is a contagion.

The only sure bulwark is continuing liberty is a government strong enough to protect the interests of the people, and a people strong enough and well enough informed o maintain its sovereign control over its government.

## FRANKLIN D ROOSEVELT
## 1882-1945

Franklin Delano Roosevelt was from a rich and influential New York family.

As a young man he entered the New York state senate, and he served as assistant secretary of the navy in Woodrow Wilson's presidency from 1913 to 1921. In 1921 he suffered a serious attack of polio, and lost the use of his legs, but this was hidden from the public right to his death.

In 1933 he was elected president of the United States, and subsequently won four elections. He steered the country through the Great Depression of the 1930s, introduced the New deal for national recovery, and led the USA against Germany and Japan in World War 11.

Order is not pressure which is imposed on society from without but an equilibrium which is set up from within.

The choice of a point of view is the initial act of a culture.

The person portrayed and the portrait are two entirely different things.

The metaphor is probably the most fertile power possessed by man.

Our life is at all times and before anything else the consciousness of what we can do.

## JOSÉ ORTEGA y GASSET
## 1883-1955

A Spanish philosopher, Ortega considered that the decline and fall of western civilisation in the twentieth century was caused by the two forces of communism and fascism. Few sensible people would disagree.

Wars may be fought with weapons but they are won by men.

To be a successful soldier, you must know history.

In war nothing is impossible, provided you use audacity.

## GEORGE S PATTON
## 1885-1945

George Smith Patton was an American general in World War II. His nickname among the troops was "blood and guts."

Although not an admirable individual, Patton is the kind of person needed to win wars, if wars are to be fought. He did not understand how sensitive people could be affected by combat and fear, and he slapped a soldier he accused of cowardice. Later, Patton had to apologise.

He died in a motor accident at the end of the war.

We know too much, and are convinced of too little. Our literature is a substitute for religion, and so is our religion.

Tradition by itself is not enough; it must be perpetually criticised and brought up to date.

## T S ELIOT
## 1888-1965

Eliot was born in the United States, and was educated in the USA, France and Britain.

He was an influential poet, dramatist and critic.

In 1921 he became a British citizen and joined the Anglican Church. Much of his poetry is concerned with belief and tradition.

Among his many poems, *The Waste Land* has been, perhaps, the most influential. *The Four Quartets* charts his religious development.

Goodness, armed with power, is corrupted; and pure love without power is destroyed.

Life has no meaning except in terms of responsibility.

**REINHOLD NIEBUHR**
**1892-1971**

An American Protestant Christian who criticised the depersonalising effects of industrial society.

Political power grows out of the barrel of a gun.

War cannot for a single minute be separated from politics.

## MAO TSE-TUNG
## 1893-1976

Most individuals, no matter how great their crimes may be, have at least one saving grace.

Mao was one of the founders in 1921 of the Chinese Communist Party. In 1949 he became leader of mainland China, and soon established a ruthless dictatorship that rivalled even that of his fellow Marxist, Joseph Stalin in Russia.

Mao was responsible for millions of deaths. He had no saving graces.

The time to stop a revolution is at the beginning, not the end.

Those who corrupt the public mind are just as evil as those who steal from the public purse.

Democracy cannot be saved by supermen, but only by the unswerving devotion and goodness of millions of little men.

## ADLAI STEVENSON
## 1900-1965

Stevenson twice stood for the presidency of the United States, and lost both times to Dwight D Eisenhower.

He was witty, educated, sophisticated and a bachelor. The American people preferred a safe, unimaginative retired general to lead them for eight years. Perhaps they were right.

Hell is – other people!

Existence is a repletion which man can never abandon.

Things are entirely what they appear to be – and behind them, there is nothing.

Man can will nothing until he has first understood that he must count on no one but himself.

## JEAN-PAUL SARTRE
## 1905-1980

Sartre was a man of many parts. He was a philosopher, political activist, novelist, essayist and playwright.

As a philosopher he was the chief exponent in Europe of the philosophy of Existentialism. He sought to reconcile Existentialism with Marxism, to the satisfaction of neither group.

Sartre lived with Simone de Beauvoir, also a writer of note and passion. His autobiography, *Les Mots*, (Words) is worth reading. Sartre spent his life with words.

A musician must make music, an artist must paint, a poet must write, if he is to be ultimately at peace with himself. What a man can be, he must be.

## ABRAHAM MASLOW
## 1908-1970

Abraham Maslow was born. Brooklyn, New York city. He was a founder of humanistic psychology in the 1960s, along with Carl Rogers, Rollo May, and others. They advanced their movement as a "third force" that provided an alternative to the schools of behaviourism and psychoanalysis.

Maslow first became known for his description of the "hierarchy of prepotency" in human motivations. Observing that "man is a wanting animal" and that one desire is no sooner satisfied than another takes its place, he noted sense and order in the succession of motives. In the relatively rare individuals in whom all lower needs are satisfied a new motive can be observed, the drive for self-actualisation.

## OTHER BOOKS FROM STRAND

The Strand Book of......Memorable Last Words
The Strand Book of......Memorable Movies
The Strand Book of......Memorable Books

## NONFICTION

Storm Over Kabul: Afghanistan, the Cockpit of Asia.
Pakistan at the Crossroads: Democracy or Islam?

## EDUCATION

Personalized Learning: Education for the 21$^{st}$ Century

## FICTION

| | |
|---|---|
| After Bolivar | Charles Markham |
| A Random Beach | James Collier |
| The Path of the Gods | Joseph Geraci |

Strand Publishing UK can be contacted by email. Please check our website for details:
www.strandpublishing.co.uk

Ideas for books are always welcome. Check our guidelines on the web page.